MznLnx

Missing Links Exam Preps

Exam Prep for

Precalculus

Faires, DeFranza, 3rd Edition

The MznLnx Exam Prep is your link from the texbook and lecture to your exams.
The MznLnx Exam Preps are unauthorized and comprehensive reviews of your textbooks.

All material provided by MznLnx and Rico Publications (c) 2010
Textbook publishers and textbook authors do not particpate in or contribute to these reviews.

MznLnx

Rico
Publications

Exam Prep for Precalculus
3rd Edition
Faires, DeFranza

Publisher: Raymond Houge
Assistant Editor: Michael Rouger
Text and Cover Designer: Lisa Buckner
Marketing Manager: Sara Swagger
Project Manager, Editorial Production: Jerry Emerson
Art Director: Vernon Lowerui

Product Manager: Dave Mason
Editorial Assitant: Rachel Guzmanji
Pedagogy: Debra Long
Cover Image: Jim Reed/Getty Images
Text and Cover Printer: City Printing, Inc.
Compositor: Media Mix, Inc.

(c) 2010 Rico Publications
ALL RIGHTS RESERVED. No part of this work covered by the copyright may be reproduced or used in any form or by an means--graphic, electronic, or mechanical, including photocopying, recording, taping, Web distribution, information storage, and retrieval systems, or in any other manner--without the written permission of the publisher.

Printed in the United States
ISBN:

For more information about our products, contact us at:
Dave.Mason@RicoPublications.com

For permission to use material from this text or product, submit a request online to:
Dave.Mason@RicoPublications.com

Contents

CHAPTER 1
  FUNCTIONS — 1
CHAPTER 2
  NEW FUNCTIONS FROM OLD — 23
CHAPTER 3
  ALGEBRAIC FUNCTIONS — 30
CHAPTER 4
  TRIGONOMETRIC FUNCTIONS — 41
CHAPTER 5
  EXPONENTIAL AND LOGARITHM FUNCTIONS — 52
CHAPTER 6
  CONIC SECTIONS, POLAR COORDINATES, AND PARAMETRIC EQUATIONS — 60
ANSWER KEY — 72

TO THE STUDENT

COMPREHENSIVE

The *MznLnx* Exam Prep series is designed to help you pass your exams. Editors at MznLnx review your textbooks and then prepare these practice exams to help you master the textbook material. Unlike study guides, workbooks, and practice tests provided by the texbook publisher and textbook authors, *MznLnx* gives you **all** of the material in each chapter in exam form, not just samples, so you can be sure to nail your exam.

MECHANICAL

The MznLnx Exam Prep series creates exams that will help you learn the subject matter as well as test you on your understanding. Each question is designed to help you master the concept. Just working through the exams, you gain an understanding of the subject--its a simple mechanical process that produces success.

INTEGRATED STUDY GUIDE AND REVIEW

MznLnx is not just a set of exams designed to test you, its also a comprehensive review of the subject content. Each exam question is also a review of the concept, making sure that you will get the answer correct without having to go to other sources of material. You learn as you go! Its the easiest way to pass an exam.

HUMOR

Studying can be tedious and dry. MznLnx's instructional design includes moderate humor within the exam questions on occassion, to break the tedium and revitalize the brain

Chapter 1. FUNCTIONS

1. The _____ are the set of numbers consisting of the natural numbers including 0 and their negatives. They are numbers that can be written without a fractional or decimal component, and fall within the set {... −2, −1, 0, 1, 2, ...}.
   a. A chemical equation
   b. A posteriori
   c. A Mathematical Theory of Communication
   d. Integers

2. In mathematics, a _____ can mean either an element of the set {1, 2, 3, ...} or an element of the set {0, 1, 2, 3, ...}. The latter is especially preferred in mathematical logic, set theory, and computer science.

   _____s have two main purposes: they can be used for counting, and they can be used for ordering.

   a. Strong partition cardinal
   b. Cardinal numbers
   c. Suslin cardinal
   d. Natural number

3. In general, an object is complete if nothing needs to be added to it. This notion is made more specific in various fields.

   In logic, semantic _____ is the converse of soundness for formal systems.

   a. Set theory
   b. Giuseppe Peano
   c. Logical equality
   d. Completeness

4. In mathematics, a _____ is a number which can be expressed as a ratio of two integers. Non-integer _____s are usually written as the vulgar fraction $\frac{a}{b}$, where b is not zero. a is called the numerator, and b the denominator.
   a. Rational number
   b. Tally marks
   c. Minkowski distance
   d. Pre-algebra

5. In mathematics, the _____s may be described informally in several different ways. The _____s include both rational numbers, such as 42 and −23/129, and irrational numbers, such as pi and the square root of two; or, a _____ can be given by an infinite decimal representation, such as 2.4871773339...., where the digits continue in some way; or, the _____s may be thought of as points on an infinitely long number line.

Chapter 1. FUNCTIONS

These descriptions of the _____s, while intuitively accessible, are not sufficiently rigorous for the purposes of pure mathematics.

a. Minkowski distance
b. Tally marks
c. Real number
d. Pre-algebra

6. In mathematics, an inequality is a statement about the relative size or order of two objects. For example 14 > 10, or 14 is _____ 10. The notation a > b means that a is _____ b and 'a' would be to the right of 'b' on a number line.

a. Greater than
b. FKG inequality
c. Cauchy-Schwarz inequality
d. Minkowski inequality

7. In mathematics, an _____ is a statement about the relative size or order of two objects, or about whether they are the same or not

- The notation a < b means that a is less than b.
- The notation a > b means that a is greater than b.
- The notation a ≠ b means that a is not equal to b, but does not say that one is bigger than the other or even that they can be compared in size.

In all these cases, a is not equal to b, hence, '_____'.

These relations are known as strict _____

- The notation a ≤ b means that a is less than or equal to b;
- The notation a ≥ b means that a is greater than or equal to b;

An additional use of the notation is to show that one quantity is much greater than another, normally by several orders of magnitude.

- The notation a << b means that a is much less than b.
- The notation a >> b means that a is much greater than b.

If the sense of the _____ is the same for all values of the variables for which its members are defined, then the _____ is called an 'absolute' or 'unconditional' _____. If the sense of an _____ holds only for certain values of the variables involved, but is reversed or destroyed for other values of the variables, it is called a conditional _____.

An _____ may appear unsolvable because it only states whether a number is larger or smaller than another number; but it is possible to apply the same operations for equalities to inequalities. For example, to find x for the _____ 10x > 23 one would divide 23 by 10.

a. A chemical equation
b. A posteriori
c. Inequality
d. A Mathematical Theory of Communication

8. In mathematics, a _____ is a set of real numbers with the property that any number that lies between two numbers in the set is also included in the set. For example, the set of all numbers x satisfying $0 \leq x \leq 1$ is an _____ which contains 0 and 1, as well as all numbers between them. Other examples of _____s are the set of all real numbers $\mathbb{R}$, the set of all positive real numbers, and the empty set.

a. Interval
b. Order
c. Annihilator
d. Ideal

9. In mathematics, the _____ of two sets A and B is the set that contains all elements of A that also belong to B, but no other elements.

For explanation of the symbols used in this article, refer to the table of mathematical symbols.

The _____ of A and B

The _____ of A and B is written 'A ∩ B'. Formally:

   x is an element of A ∩ B if and only if
   - x is an element of A and
   - x is an element of B.

For example:
   - The _____ of the sets {1, 2, 3} and {2, 3, 4} is {2, 3}.
   - The number 9 is not in the _____ of the set of prime numbers {2, 3, 5, 7, 11, â€¦} and the set of odd numbers {1, 3, 5, 7, 9, 11, â€¦}.

If the _____ of two sets A and B is empty, that is they have no elements in common, then they are said to be disjoint, denoted: A ∩ B = Ø. For example the sets {1, 2} and {3, 4} are disjoint, written
{1, 2} ∩ {3, 4} = Ø.

a. Order
b. Intersection
c. Advice
d. Erlang

10. _____ is the notation in which permitted values for a variable are expressed as ranging over a certain interval; "5 < x < 9" is an example of the application of _____.
a. Infinity
b. A Mathematical Theory of Communication
c. Implicit differentiation
d. Interval notation

11. _____ is the state of being greater than any finite number, however large.
a. Implicit differentiation
b. Interval notation
c. Infinity
d. A Mathematical Theory of Communication

12. The mathematical concept of a _____ expresses the intuitive idea of deterministic dependence between two quantities, one of which is viewed as primary and the other as secondary. A _____ then is a way to associate a unique output for each input of a specified type, for example, a real number or an element of a given set.
a. Grill
b. Coherent
c. Going up
d. Function

13. In set theory, the term _____ refers to a set operation used in the convergence of set elements to form a resultant set containing the elements of both sets. As a simple example, a _____ of two disjoint sets, which do not have elements in common results in a set containing all elements from both sets. A Venn diagram representing the _____ of sets A and B.
a. UES
b. Event
c. Introduction
d. Union

Chapter 1. FUNCTIONS

14. In mathematics, the _____ of a real number is its numerical value without regard to its sign. So, for example, 3 is the _____ of both 3 and −3.

The _____ of a number a is denoted by | a |.

Generalizations of the _____ for real numbers occur in a wide variety of mathematical settings.

   a. A Mathematical Theory of Communication
   b. Area hyperbolic functions
   c. Absolute value
   d. A chemical equation

15. In mathematics, a _____ is, informally, an infinitely vast and infinitely thin sheet. _____s may be thought of as objects in some higher dimensional space, or they may be considered without any outside space, as in the setting of Euclidean geometry
   a. Plane
   b. Blocking
   c. Bandwidth
   d. Group

16. _____ is a temperature scale that is named after the German physicist Daniel Gabriel _____, who proposed it in 1724.

In this scale, the freezing point of water is 32 degrees _____ and the boiling point 212 °F, placing the boiling and freezing points of water exactly 180 degrees apart. A degree on the _____ scale is 1/180th part of the interval between the ice point and the boiling point.

   a. 1-center problem
   b. Fahrenheit
   c. 2-3 heap
   d. 120-cell

17. In quantum field theory and statistical mechanics in the thermodynamic limit, a system with a global symmetry can have more than one phase. For parameters where the symmetry is spontaneously broken, the system is said to be _____. When the global symmetry is unbroken the system is disordered.

a. Ursell function
b. Einstein relation
c. Isoenthalpic-isobaric ensemble
d. Ordered

18. In mathematics, an _____ is a collection of objects having two coordinates (or entries or projections), such that one can always uniquely determine the object, which is the first coordinate (or first entry or left projection) of the pair as well as the second coordinate (or second entry or right projection.) If the first coordinate is a and the second is b, the usual notation for an _____ is (a, b.) The pair is 'ordered' in that (a, b) differs from (b, a) unless a = b.
a. A chemical equation
b. A posteriori
c. A Mathematical Theory of Communication
d. Ordered pair

19. In mathematics, the _____ of a Euclidean space is a special point, usually denoted by the letter O, used as a fixed point of reference for the geometry of the surrounding space. In a Cartesian coordinate system, the _____ is the point where the axes of the system intersect. In Euclidean geometry, the _____ may be chosen freely as any convenient point of reference.
a. OMAC
b. Interval
c. Autonomous system
d. Origin

20. The _____ is the horizontal axis of a two-dimensional plot in the Cartesian coordinate system, that is typically pointed to the right. Also known as a right-handed coordinate system.
a. 120-cell
b. 2-3 heap
c. X-axis
d. 1-center problem

21. In reference to a 2D and 3D plane, the _____ is the vertical height of a 2D or 3D object.
a. 1-center problem
b. 120-cell
c. Y-axis
d. 2-3 heap

Chapter 1. FUNCTIONS

22. The x-axis is the horizontal axis of a two- dimensional plot in the _____, that is typically pointed to the right. Also known as a right-handed coordinate system.

   a. 2-3 heap
   b. 120-cell
   c. 1-center problem
   d. Cartesian coordinate system

23. In mathematics, the _____ or Pythagoras' theorem is a relation in Euclidean geometry among the three sides of a right triangle. The theorem is named after the Greek mathematician Pythagoras, who by tradition is credited with its discovery and proof, although it is often argued that knowledge of the theory predates him.. The theorem is as follows:

In any right triangle, the area of the square whose side is the hypotenuse is equal to the sum of the areas of the squares whose sides are the two legs.

   a. 1-center problem
   b. 2-3 heap
   c. 120-cell
   d. Pythagorean Theorem

24. In mathematics, a _____ is a statement that can be proved on the basis of explicitly stated or previously agreed assumptions.
   a. Boolean function
   b. Logical value
   c. Disjunction introduction
   d. Theorem

25. A _____ is a simple shape of Euclidean geometry consisting of those points in a plane which are at a constant distance, called the radius, from a fixed point, called the center. A _____ with center A is sometimes denoted by the symbol A.

A chord of a _____ is a line segment whose two endpoints lie on the _____.

   a. Circumcircle
   b. Circular segment
   c. Malfatti circles
   d. Circle

26. _____, also sometimes known as standard form or as exponential notation, is a way of writing numbers that accommodates values too large or small to be conveniently written in standard decimal notation. _____ has a number of useful properties and is often favored by scientists, mathematicians and engineers, who work with such numbers.

In _____, numbers are written in the form:

$$a \times 10^b$$

   a. Leading zero
   b. Radix point
   c. 1-center problem
   d. Scientific notation

27. In mathematics, a _____ is a circle with a unit radius. Frequently, especially in trigonometry, 'the' _____ is the circle of radius 1 centered at the origin in the Cartesian coordinate system in the Euclidean plane. The _____ is often denoted S^1; the generalization to higher dimensions is the unit sphere.
   a. Inscribed angle theorem
   b. Unit circle
   c. Open unit disk
   d. Excircle

28. In mathematics, _____ are a method of defining a curve. A simple kinematical example is when one uses a time parameter to determine the position, velocity, and other information about a body in motion.

Abstractly, a relation is given in the form of an equation, and it is shown also to be the image of functions from items such as R^n.

   a. Laplace operator
   b. Multipole moment
   c. Differential operator
   d. Parametric equations

29. _____ is an algebraic technique used to solve quadratic equations, in analytic geometry for determining the shapes of graphs, and in calculus for computing integrals. The essential objective is to reduce a quadratic polynomial in a variable in an equation or expression to a squared polynomial of linear order. This can reduce an equation or integral to one that is more easily solved or evaluated.

Chapter 1. FUNCTIONS 9

a. Permanent of a matrix
b. Monomial basis
c. Relation algebra
d. Completing the square

30. In mathematics, the term _____ has several different important meanings:

- An _____ is an equality that remains true regardless of the values of any variables that appear within it, to distinguish it from an equality which is true under more particular conditions. For this, the 'triple bar' symbol ≡ is sometimes used.
- In algebra, an _____ or _____ element of a set S with a binary operation Â· is an element e that, when combined with any element x of S, produces that same x. That is, eÂ·x = xÂ·e = x for all x in S.
  - The _____ function from a set S to itself, often denoted id or id$_S$, s the function such that i = x for all x in S. This function serves as the _____ element in the set of all functions from S to itself with respect to function composition.
  - In linear algebra, the _____ matrix of size n is the n-by-n square matrix with ones on the main diagonal and zeros elsewhere. This matrix serves as the _____ with respect to matrix multiplication.

A common example of the first meaning is the trigonometric _____

$$\sin^2 \theta + \cos^2 \theta = 1$$

which is true for all real values of θ, as opposed to

$$\cos \theta = 1,$$

which is true only for some values of θ, not all. For example, the latter equation is true when $\theta = 0$, false when $\theta = 2$

The concepts of 'additive _____' and 'multiplicative _____' are central to the Peano axioms. The number 0 is the 'additive _____' for integers, real numbers, and complex numbers. For the real numbers, for all $a \in \mathbb{R}$,

$$0 + a = a,$$

$$a + 0 = a, \text{ and}$$

$$0 + 0 = 0.$$

Similarly, The number 1 is the 'multiplicative _____' for integers, real numbers, and complex numbers.

a. ARIA
b. Intersection
c. Identity
d. Action

31. In mathematics, the _____ is a conic section, the intersection of a right circular conical surface and a plane parallel to a generating straight line of that surface. Given a point and a line that lie in a plane, the locus of points in that plane that are equidistant to them is a _____.

A particular case arises when the plane is tangent to the conical surface of a circle.

   a. Matrix representation of conic sections
   b. Dandelin sphere
   c. Directrix
   d. Parabola

32. _____ generally conveys two primary meanings. The first is an imprecise sense of harmonious or aesthetically-pleasing proportionality and balance; such that it reflects beauty or perfection. The second meaning is a precise and well-defined concept of balance or 'patterned self-similarity' that can be demonstrated or proved according to the rules of a formal system: by geometry, through physics or otherwise.
   a. Symmetry breaking
   b. Symmetry
   c. Tessellation
   d. Molecular symmetry

33. A _____ is a software program that facilitates symbolic mathematics. The core functionality of a CAS is manipulation of mathematical expressions in symbolic form.

Chapter 1. FUNCTIONS

The symbolic manipulations supported typically include

- simplification to the smallest possible expression or some standard form, including automatic simplification with assumptions and simplification with constraints
- substitution of symbolic, functors or numeric values for expressions
- change of form of expressions: expanding products and powers, partial and full factorization, rewriting as partial fractions, constraint satisfaction, rewriting trigonometric functions as exponentials, etc.
- partial and total differentiation
- symbolic constrained and unconstrained global optimization
- solution of linear and some non-linear equations over various domains
- solution of some differential and difference equations
- taking some limits
- some indefinite and definite integration, including multidimensional integrals
- integral transforms
- arbitrary-precision numeric operations
- Series operations such as expansion, summation and products
- matrix operations including products, inverses, etc.
- display of mathematical expressions in two-dimensional mathematical form, often using typesetting systems similar to TeX
- add-ons for use in applied mathematics such as physics packages for physical computation
- plotting graphs and parametric plots of functions in two and three dimensions, and animating them
- APIs for linking it on an external program such as a database, or using in a programming language to use the
- drawing charts and diagrams
- string manipulation such as matching and searching
- statistical computation
- Theorem proving and verification
- graphic production and editing such as CGI and signal processing as image processing
- sound synthesis

Many also include a programming language, allowing users to implement their own algorithms.

Some _____s focus on a specific area of application; these are typically developed in academia and are free.

a. 2-3 heap
b. 1-center problem
c. 120-cell
d. Computer algebra system

34. A _____ typically refers to a class of handheld calculators that are capable of plotting graphs, solving simultaneous equations, and performing numerous other tasks with variables. Most popular _____s are also programmable, allowing the user to create customized programs, typically for scientific/engineering and education applications. Due to their large displays intended for graphing, they can also accommodate several lines of text and calculations at a time.
   a. Support vector machines
   b. Genus
   c. Bump mapping
   d. Graphing calculator

35. A _____ is a device for performing mathematical calculations, distinguished from a computer by having a limited problem solving ability and an interface optimized for interactive calculation rather than programming. _____s can be hardware or software, and mechanical or electronic, and are often built into devices such as PDAs or mobile phones.

Modern electronic _____s are generally small, digital, and usually inexpensive.

   a. 1-center problem
   b. Calculator
   c. 2-3 heap
   d. 120-cell

36. In geometry, a _____ is defined as a quadrilateral where all four of its angles are right angles.
   a. Point group in two dimensions
   b. Polytope
   c. Cantor-Dedekind axiom
   d. Rectangle

37. _____ and independent variables refer to values that change in relationship to each other. The _____ are those that are observed to change in response to the independent variables. The independent variables are those that are deliberately manipulated to invoke a change in the _____.
   a. Yates analysis
   b. Dependent variables
   c. Round robin test
   d. Steiner system

38. Dependent variables and _____ refer to values that change in relationship to each other. The dependent variables are those that are observed to change in response to the _____. The _____ are those that are deliberately manipulated to invoke a change in the dependent variables.

Chapter 1. FUNCTIONS 13

a. One-factor-at-a-time method
b. Experimental design diagram
c. Operational confound
d. Independent variables

39. In mathematics, especially in the area of abstract algebra known as ring theory, a _____ is a ring with 0 ≠ 1 such that ab = 0 implies that either a = 0 or b = 0. That is, it is a nontrivial ring without left or right zero divisors. A commutative _____ is called an integral _____.
   a. Modular representation theory
   b. Left primitive ring
   c. Simple ring
   d. Domain

40. An _____ is an artifact, usually two-dimensional (a picture), that has a similar appearance to some subject--usually a physical object or a person.

_____s may be two-dimensional, such as a photograph, screen display, and as well as a three-dimensional, such as a statue. They may be captured by optical devices--such as cameras, mirrors, lenses, telescopes, microscopes, etc.

   a. A Mathematical Theory of Communication
   b. A chemical equation
   c. A posteriori
   d. Image

41. In mathematics, an algebraic group G contains a unique maximal normal solvable subgroup; and this subgroup is closed. Its identity component is called the _____ of G.
   a. Composite
   b. Radical
   c. Barycentric coordinates
   d. Block size

42. In descriptive statistics, the _____ is the length of the smallest interval which contains all the data. It is calculated by subtracting the smallest observations from the greatest and provides an indication of statistical dispersion.

It is measured in the same units as the data.

Chapter 1. FUNCTIONS

a. Bandwidth
b. Class
c. Range
d. Kernel

43. In mathematics, a _____ of a number x is a number r such that r² = x, or, in other words, a number r whose square is x. Every non-negative real number x has a unique non-negative _____, called the principal _____, which is denoted with a radical symbol as $\sqrt{x}$, or, using exponent notation, as x^(1/2). For example, the principal _____ of 9 is 3, denoted $\sqrt{9}$ = 3, because 3² = 3 × 3 = 9.

a. Double exponential
b. Hyperbolic functions
c. Square root
d. Multiplicative inverse

44. In vascular plants, the _____ is the organ of a plant body that typically lies below the surface of the soil. This is not always the case, however, since a _____ can also be aerial (that is, growing above the ground) or aerating (that is, growing up above the ground or especially above water.) Furthermore, a stem normally occurring below ground is not exceptional either

a. 1-center problem
b. Root
c. 2-3 heap
d. 120-cell

45. An _____ of a real-valued function y = f(x) is a curve which describes the behavior of f as either x or y tends to infinity.

In other words, as one moves along the graph of f(x) in some direction, the distance between it and the _____ eventually becomes smaller than any distance that one may specify.

If a curve A has the curve B as an _____, one says that A is asymptotic to B. Similarly B is asymptotic to A, so A and B are called asymptotic.

a. Improper integral
b. Infinite product
c. Isoperimetric dimension
d. Asymptote

46. To define the derivative of a distribution, we first consider the case of a differentiable and integrable function f : R → R. If φ is a _____, then we have

$$\int_{\mathbf{R}} f'\varphi\, dx = -\int_{\mathbf{R}} f\varphi'\, dx$$

using integration by parts (note that φ is zero outside of a bounded set and that therefore no boundary values have to be taken into account.) This suggests that if S is a distribution, we should define its derivative S' by

$$\langle S', \varphi \rangle = -\langle S, \varphi' \rangle.$$

- a. Generalized functions
- b. Hyperfunction
- c. Schwartz kernel theorem
- d. Test Function

47. In mathematics, a _____ is a function whose definition is dependent on the value of the independent variable. Mathematically, a real-valued function f of a real variable x is a relationship whose definition is given differently on disjoint subsets of its domain

The word piecewise is also used to describe any property of a _____ that holds for each piece but may not hold for the whole domain of the function.

- a. High-dimensional model representation
- b. Piecewise-defined function
- c. Surjective
- d. Glide reflection

48. In mathematics, _____ and undefined are used to explain whether or not expressions have meaningful, sensible, and unambiguous values. Not all branches of mathematics come to the same conclusion.

The following expressions are undefined in all contexts, but remarks in the analysis section may apply.

- a. Plugging in
- b. Defined
- c. LHS
- d. Toy model

49. In mathematics, a _____ is the end result of a division problem. It can also be expressed as the number of times the divisor divides into the dividend.
   a. Limiting
   b. Marginal cost
   c. Notation
   d. Quotient

50. In mathematics, even functions and _____s are functions which satisfy particular symmetry relations, with respect to taking additive inverses. They are important in many areas of mathematical analysis, especially the theory of power series and Fourier series. They are named for the parity of the powers of the power functions which satisfy each condition: the function f(x) = x^n is an even function if n is an even integer, and it is an _____ if n is an odd integer.
   a. A chemical equation
   b. A posteriori
   c. A Mathematical Theory of Communication
   d. Odd function

51. A _____ is a type of display using Cartesian coordinates to display values for two variables for a set of data. The data is displayed as a collection of points, each having the value of one variable determining the position on the horizontal axis and the value of the other variable determining the position on the vertical axis. A _____ is also called a scatter chart, scatter diagram and scatter graph.
   a. Scatter plot
   b. 1-center problem
   c. 2-3 heap
   d. 120-cell

52. _____ is used to describe the steepness, incline, gradient, or grade of a straight line. A higher _____ value indicates a steeper incline. The _____ is defined as the ratio of the 'rise' divided by the 'run' between two points on a line, or in other words, the ratio of the altitude change to the horizontal distance between any two points on the line.
   a. Cognitively Guided Instruction
   b. Point plotting
   c. Slope
   d. Number line

53. A _____ is an algebraic equation in which each term is either a constant or the product of a constant and a single variable. _____s can have one, two, three or more variables.

_____s occur with great regularity in applied mathematics.

Chapter 1. FUNCTIONS   17

  a. Linear equation
  b. Quartic equation
  c. Quadratic equation
  d. Difference of two squares

54. A _____ is is a graphical technique for presenting a data set drawn by hand or produced by a mechanical or electronic plotter. It is a graph depicting the relationship between two or more variables used, for instance, in visualising scientific data.

_____s play an important role in statistics and data analysis.

  a. C-35
  b. Dini
  c. Lattice
  d. Plot

55. The _____ expresses the fact that the difference in the y coordinate between two points on a line that is, y − y1 is proportional to the difference in the x coordinate that is, x − x1. The proportionality constant is m (the slope of the line.
  a. Square function
  b. Rubin Causal Model
  c. Cobb-Douglas
  d. Point-slope form

56. _____ is a form where m is the slope of the line and b is the y-intercept, which is the y-coordinate of the point where the line crosses the y axis. This can be seen by letting x = 0, which immediately gives y = b.
  a. Separable extension
  b. Dynamical system
  c. Commutative law
  d. Slope-intercept form

57. In mathematics, specifically in combinatorial commutative algebra, a convex lattice polytope P is called _____ if it has the following property: given any positive integer n, every lattice point of the dilation nP, obtained from P by scaling its vertices by the factor n and taking the convex hull of the resulting points, can be written as the sum of exactly n lattice points in P. This property plays an important role in the theory of toric varieties, where it corresponds to projective normality of the toric variety determined by P.

The simplex in R^k with the vertices at the origin and along the unit coordinate vectors is _____.

a. Hypercube
b. Polytetrahedron
c. Normal
d. Demihypercubes

58. In the two-dimensional case, a _____ perpendicularly intersects the tangent line to a curve at a given point.

The normal is often used in computer graphics to determine a surface's orientation toward a light source for flat shading, or the orientation of each of the corners (vertices) to mimic a curved surface with Phong shading.

For a polygon (such as a triangle), a surface normal can be calculated as the vector cross product of two (non-parallel) edges of the polygon.

a. Homoeoid
b. Normal line
c. Cross-cap
d. Parametric surface

59. A _____ of a curve is the envelope of a family of congruent circles centered on the curve. It generalises the concept of _____ lines.

It is sometimes called the offset curve but the term 'offset' often refers also to translation.

a. Parallel
b. Bifolium
c. Cycloid
d. Cissoid

60. The existence and properties of _____ are the basis of Euclid's parallel postulate. _____ are two lines on the same plane that do not intersect even assuming that lines extend to infinity in either direction.

a. Vertical translation
b. Parallel lines
c. Spidron
d. Square wheel

Chapter 1. FUNCTIONS

61. In mathematics, the _____ is an approach to finding a particular solution to certain inhomogeneous ordinary differential equations and recurrence relations. It is closely related to the annihilator method, but instead of using a particular kind of differential operator in order to find the best possible form of the particular solution, a 'guess' is made as to the appropriate form, which is then tested by differentiating the resulting equation. In this sense, the _____ is less formal but more intuitive than the annihilator method.

a. Phase line
b. Differential algebraic equations
c. Linear differential equation
d. Method of undetermined coefficients

62. Suppose f is a function. Then the line y = a is a _____ for f if

$$\lim_{x \to \infty} f(x) = a \text{ or } \lim_{x \to -\infty} f(x) = a.$$

Intuitively, this means that f(x) can be made as close as desired to a by making x big enough. How big is big enough depends on how close one wishes to make f(x) to a.

a. 120-cell
b. 2-3 heap
c. 1-center problem
d. Horizontal asymptote

63. In calculus, a function f defined on a subset of the real numbers with real values is called monotonic (also monotonically increasing or non-_____), if for all x and y such that x ≤ y one has f(x) ≤ f(y), so f preserves the order. In layman's terms, the sign of the slope is always positive (the curve tending upwards) or zero (i.e., non-_____, or asymptotic, or depicted as a horizontal, flat line) Likewise, a function is called monotonically _____ (non-increasing) if, whenever x ≤ y, then f(x) ≥ f(y), so it reverses the order.

a. Circular convolution
b. Decreasing
c. Tensor product of Hilbert spaces
d. Dual pair

64. A _____, in mathematics, is a polynomial function of the form $f(x) = ax^2 + bx + c$, where $a \neq 0$. The graph of a _____ is a parabola whose major axis is parallel to the y-axis.

The expression $ax^2 + bx + c$ in the definition of a _____ is a polynomial of degree 2 or a 2nd degree polynomial, because the highest exponent of x is 2.

a. Quadratic function
b. Laguerre polynomials
c. Discriminant
d. Multivariate division algorithm

65. _____ is the interpreting of the meaning of a text and the subsequent production of an equivalent text, likewise called a '_____,' that communicates the same message in another language. The text to be translated is called the 'source text,' and the language that it is to be translated into is called the 'target language'; the final product is sometimes called the 'target text.'

_____ must take into account constraints that include context, the rules of grammar of the two languages, their writing conventions, and their idioms. A common misconception is that there exists a simple word-for-word correspondence between any two languages, and that _____ is a straightforward mechanical process; such a word-for-word _____, however, cannot take into account context, grammar, conventions, and idioms.

a. 120-cell
b. 2-3 heap
c. 1-center problem
d. Translation

66. In geometry, a _____ is a special kind of point, usually a corner of a polygon, polyhedron, or higher dimensional polytope. In the geometry of curves a _____ is a point of where the first derivative of curvature is zero. In graph theory, a _____ is the fundamental unit out of which graphs are formed
a. Crib
b. Vertex
c. Duality
d. Dini

67. In geometry and trigonometry, an _____ is the figure formed by two rays sharing a common endpoint, called the vertex of the _____. The magnitude of the _____ is the 'amount of rotation' that separates the two rays, and can be measured by considering the length of circular arc swept out when one ray is rotated about the vertex to coincide with the other. Where there is no possibility of confusion, the term '_____' is used interchangeably for both the geometric configuration itself and for its angular magnitude.
a. Angle
b. A posteriori
c. A Mathematical Theory of Communication
d. A chemical equation

68. In function graphing, a _____ is a related graph which, for every point (x, y); has a y value which differs from another graph, by exactly some constant c. For example, the antiderivatives of a family are _____s of each other.
   a. Parallel postulate
   b. Central angle
   c. Complementary angles
   d. Vertical Translation

69. In mathematics, a _____ is a polynomial equation of the second degree. The general form is

$$ax^2 + bx + c = 0,$$

where a ≠ 0.

The letters a, b, and c are called coefficients: the quadratic coefficient a is the coefficient of x^2, the linear coefficient b is the coefficient of x, and c is the constant coefficient, also called the free term or constant term.

   a. Difference of two squares
   b. Linear equation
   c. Quartic equation
   d. Quadratic equation

70. In algebra, the _____ of a polynomial with real or complex coefficients is a certain expression in the coefficients of the polynomial which is equal to zero if and only if the polynomial has a multiple root in the complex numbers. For example, the _____ of the quadratic polynomial

$$ax^2 + bx + c \text{ is } b^2 - 4ac.$$

The _____ of the cubic polynomial

$$ax^3 + bx^2 + cx + d \text{ is } b^2c^2 - 4ac^3 - 4b^3d - 27a^2d^2 + 18abcd.$$

   a. Jacobian conjecture
   b. Boubaker polynomial
   c. Square-free polynomial
   d. Discriminant

71. A quadratic equation with real solutions, called roots, which may be real or complex, is given by the _____: $x = {-b \pm \sqrt{b^2 - 4ac}}/{...}$

Chapter 1. FUNCTIONS

a. Quotient
b. Differential Algebra
c. Quadratic formula
d. Parametric continuity

72. In mathematics and in the sciences, a _____ (plural: _____e, formulæ or _____s) is a concise way of expressing information symbolically (as in a mathematical or chemical _____), or a general relationship between quantities. One of many famous _____e is Albert Einstein's E = mc² (see special relativity

In mathematics, a _____ is a key to solve an equation with variables. For example, the problem of determining the volume of a sphere is one that requires a significant amount of integral calculus to solve.

a. 120-cell
b. 1-center problem
c. 2-3 heap
d. Formula

73. In mathematics, a _____ is an expression constructed from variables and constants, using the operations of addition, subtraction, multiplication, and constant non-negative whole number exponents. For example, $x^2 - 4x + 7$ is a _____, but $x^2 - 4/x + 7x^{3/2}$ is not, because its second term involves division by the variable x and also because its third term contains an exponent that is not a whole number.

_____s are one of the most important concepts in algebra and throughout mathematics and science.

a. Semifield
b. Group extension
c. Coimage
d. Polynomial

74. In mathematics, a _____ is a constant multiplicative factor of a certain object. For example, in the expression $9x^2$, the _____ of x^2 is 9.

The object can be such things as a variable, a vector, a function, etc.

a. Multivariate division algorithm
b. Stability radius
c. Fibonacci polynomials
d. Coefficient

Chapter 2. NEW FUNCTIONS FROM OLD

1. In mathematics, the _____ of a real number is its numerical value without regard to its sign. So, for example, 3 is the _____ of both 3 and −3.

   The _____ of a number a is denoted by | a |.

   Generalizations of the _____ for real numbers occur in a wide variety of mathematical settings.

   a. A chemical equation
   b. Absolute value
   c. Area hyperbolic functions
   d. A Mathematical Theory of Communication

2. The mathematical concept of a _____ expresses the intuitive idea of deterministic dependence between two quantities, one of which is viewed as primary and the other as secondary. A _____ then is a way to associate a unique output for each input of a specified type, for example, a real number or an element of a given set.

   a. Going up
   b. Coherent
   c. Function
   d. Grill

3. In mathematics, a _____ of a number x is a number r such that r^2 = x, or, in other words, a number r whose square is x. Every non-negative real number x has a unique non-negative _____, called the principal _____, which is denoted with a radical symbol as $\sqrt{x}$, or, using exponent notation, as $x^{1/2}$. For example, the principal _____ of 9 is 3, denoted $\sqrt{9}$ = 3, because 3^2 = 3 × 3 = 9.

   a. Hyperbolic functions
   b. Multiplicative inverse
   c. Double exponential
   d. Square root

4. In vascular plants, the _____ is the organ of a plant body that typically lies below the surface of the soil. This is not always the case, however, since a _____ can also be aerial (that is, growing above the ground) or aerating (that is, growing up above the ground or especially above water.) Furthermore, a stem normally occurring below ground is not exceptional either

   a. 1-center problem
   b. 120-cell
   c. 2-3 heap
   d. Root

5. In mathematics and computer science, the _____ and ceiling functions map real numbers to the next lower and next higher integers.

The _____ function of a real number x, sometimes called the greatest integer or entier function, and denoted variously by [x] $\lfloor x \rfloor$, _____(x), or int(x), is a function whose value is the largest integer less than or equal to x. Formally, for all real numbers x,

$$\lfloor x \rfloor = \max\{n \in \mathbb{Z} \mid n \leq x\}.$$

For example, _____(2.9) = 2, _____(−2) = −2 and _____(−12/5) = −3.

a. Floor
b. 2-3 heap
c. 1-center problem
d. 120-cell

6. The _____ are the set of numbers consisting of the natural numbers including 0 and their negatives. They are numbers that can be written without a fractional or decimal component, and fall within the set {... −2, −1, 0, 1, 2, ...}.
a. A chemical equation
b. A Mathematical Theory of Communication
c. A posteriori
d. Integers

7. In mathematics, a _____ is the end result of a division problem. It can also be expressed as the number of times the divisor divides into the dividend.
a. Limiting
b. Marginal cost
c. Notation
d. Quotient

8. In mathematics, the _____s are an extension of the real numbers obtained by adjoining an imaginary unit, denoted i, which satisfies:

$$i^2 = -1.$$

Every _____ can be written in the form a + bi, where a and b are real numbers called the real part and the imaginary part of the _____, respectively.

Chapter 2. NEW FUNCTIONS FROM OLD

_____s are a field, and thus have addition, subtraction, multiplication, and division operations. These operations extend the corresponding operations on real numbers, although with a number of additional elegant and useful properties, e.g., negative real numbers can be obtained by squaring _____s.

  a. 120-cell
  b. Complex number
  c. Real part
  d. 1-center problem

9. In functional analysis, the _____ of a linear operator T on a Hilbert space to a subspace K is the operator

$$P_K T|_K$$

where P_K is the orthogonal projection onto K. This is a natural way to obtain an operator on K from an operator on the whole Hilbert space. If K is an invariant subspace for T, then the _____ of T to K is the restricted operator K→K sending k to Tk.

  a. Compression
  b. Dini
  c. Center
  d. Figure-eight knot

10. An _____ of a real-valued function y = f(x) is a curve which describes the behavior of f as either x or y tends to infinity.

In other words, as one moves along the graph of f(x) in some direction, the distance between it and the _____ eventually becomes smaller than any distance that one may specify.

If a curve A has the curve B as an _____, one says that A is asymptotic to B. Similarly B is asymptotic to A, so A and B are called asymptotic.

  a. Isoperimetric dimension
  b. Improper integral
  c. Asymptote
  d. Infinite product

11. In mathematics, the _____ of a Euclidean space is a special point, usually denoted by the letter O, used as a fixed point of reference for the geometry of the surrounding space. In a Cartesian coordinate system, the _____ is the point where the axes of the system intersect. In Euclidean geometry, the _____ may be chosen freely as any convenient point of reference.

a. Interval
b. Autonomous system
c. OMAC
d. Origin

12. The _____ is the horizontal axis of a two-dimensional plot in the Cartesian coordinate system, that is typically pointed to the right. Also known as a right-handed coordinate system.

a. 2-3 heap
b. 120-cell
c. 1-center problem
d. X-axis

13. In mathematics, the multiplicative inverse of a number x, denoted 1/x or x^{-1}, is the number which, when multiplied by x, yields 1. The multiplicative inverse of x is also called the _____ of x.

a. 1-center problem
b. Reciprocal
c. 2-3 heap
d. 120-cell

14. Suppose f is a function. Then the line y = a is a _____ for f if

$$\lim_{x \to \infty} f(x) = a \text{ or } \lim_{x \to -\infty} f(x) = a.$$

Intuitively, this means that f(x) can be made as close as desired to a by making x big enough. How big is big enough depends on how close one wishes to make f(x) to a.

a. 2-3 heap
b. 120-cell
c. 1-center problem
d. Horizontal asymptote

15. In reference to a 2D and 3D plane, the _____ is the vertical height of a 2D or 3D object.

Chapter 2. NEW FUNCTIONS FROM OLD

   a. 120-cell
   b. Y-axis
   c. 2-3 heap
   d. 1-center problem

16. _____ is a temperature scale that is named after the German physicist Daniel Gabriel _____, who proposed it in 1724.

In this scale, the freezing point of water is 32 degrees _____ and the boiling point 212 °F, placing the boiling and freezing points of water exactly 180 degrees apart. A degree on the _____ scale is 1/180th part of the interval between the ice point and the boiling point.

   a. 120-cell
   b. 1-center problem
   c. Fahrenheit
   d. 2-3 heap

17. An injective function is called an injection, and is also said to be a _____ (not to be confused with one-to-one correspondence, i.e. a bijective function.)

A function f that is not injective is sometimes called many-to-one. (However, this terminology is also sometimes used to mean 'single-valued', i.e. each argument is mapped to at most one value.)

   a. A Mathematical Theory of Communication
   b. A chemical equation
   c. One-to-one function
   d. A posteriori

18. In mathematics, the _____ is a test used to determine if a function is injective, surjective or bijective.

Suppose there is a function f : X → Y with a graph., and you have a horizontal line of X x Y :
$y_0 \in Y, \{(x, y_0) : x \in X\} = (X \times y_0)$.

- If the function is injective, then it can be visualized as one whose graph is never intersected by any horizontal line more than once.
- Iff f is surjective any horizontal line will intersect the graph at least at one point
- If f is bijective any horizontal line will intersect the graph at exactly one point.

This test is also used to find whether or not the inverse of the function is indeed a function as well. This is due to the reflective properties of the function over y=x.

a. Horizontal line test
b. Subset
c. Multiset
d. Disjoint sets

19. To define the derivative of a distribution, we first consider the case of a differentiable and integrable function f : R → R. If φ is a _____, then we have

$$\int_R f'\varphi\, dx = -\int_R f\varphi'\, dx$$

using integration by parts (note that φ is zero outside of a bounded set and that therefore no boundary values have to be taken into account.) This suggests that if S is a distribution, we should define its derivative S' by

$$\langle S', \varphi \rangle = -\langle S, \varphi' \rangle.$$

a. Generalized functions
b. Schwartz kernel theorem
c. Test Function
d. Hyperfunction

20. In mathematics, the _____ of a number n is the number that, when added to n, yields zero. The _____ of n is denoted −n. For example, 7 is −7, because 7 + (−7) = 0, and the _____ of −0.3 is 0.3, because −0.3 + 0.3 = 0.

a. Associativity
b. Algebraic structure
c. Arity
d. Additive inverse

21. An _____ is a function which does the reverse of a given function.

Chapter 2. NEW FUNCTIONS FROM OLD

a. Empty function
b. Inverse function
c. A Mathematical Theory of Communication
d. Empty set

22. In mathematics an _____ , a 'falling short') is a conic section, the locus of points in a plane such that the sum of the distances to two fixed points is equal to a given constant. The two fixed points are then called foci.

Another way is to define it as the path traced out by a point whose distance from a focus maintains a constant ratio less than one with its distance from a straight line not passing through the focus, called the directrix.

a. A posteriori
b. A Mathematical Theory of Communication
c. A chemical equation
d. Ellipse

Chapter 3. ALGEBRAIC FUNCTIONS

1. In mathematics, a _____ is a function whose values do not vary and thus are constant. For example, if we have the function f→ B is a _____ if f
   a. Linear operator
   b. Squeeze mapping
   c. Point reflection
   d. Constant function

2. The mathematical concept of a _____ expresses the intuitive idea of deterministic dependence between two quantities, one of which is viewed as primary and the other as secondary. A _____ then is a way to associate a unique output for each input of a specified type, for example, a real number or an element of a given set.
   a. Going up
   b. Coherent
   c. Grill
   d. Function

3. In mathematics, a _____ is an expression constructed from variables and constants, using the operations of addition, subtraction, multiplication, and constant non-negative whole number exponents. For example, $x^2 - 4x + 7$ is a _____, but $x^2 - 4/x + 7x^{3/2}$ is not, because its second term involves division by the variable x and also because its third term contains an exponent that is not a whole number.

   _____s are one of the most important concepts in algebra and throughout mathematics and science.

   a. Polynomial
   b. Group extension
   c. Coimage
   d. Semifield

4. A _____, in mathematics, is a polynomial function of the form $f(x) = ax^2 + bx + c$, where $a \neq 0$. The graph of a _____ is a parabola whose major axis is parallel to the y-axis.

   The expression $ax^2 + bx + c$ in the definition of a _____ is a polynomial of degree 2 or a 2nd degree polynomial, because the highest exponent of x is 2.

   a. Multivariate division algorithm
   b. Discriminant
   c. Laguerre polynomials
   d. Quadratic function

Chapter 3. ALGEBRAIC FUNCTIONS

5. In mathematics, a _____ is any function which can be written as the ratio of two polynomial functions. _____ of degree 2 :

$$y = \frac{x^2 - 3x - 2}{x^2 - 4}$$

In the case of one variable, x, a _____ is a function of the form

$$f(x) = \frac{P(x)}{Q(x)}$$

where P and Q are polynomial function in x and Q is not the zero polynomial. The domain of f is the set of all points x for which the denominator Q

    a. Legendre rational functions
    b. 1-center problem
    c. 120-cell
    d. Rational function

6. In mathematics, the _____ of a real number is its numerical value without regard to its sign. So, for example, 3 is the _____ of both 3 and −3.

The _____ of a number a is denoted by $|\,a\,|$.

Generalizations of the _____ for real numbers occur in a wide variety of mathematical settings.

    a. Area hyperbolic functions
    b. Absolute value
    c. A chemical equation
    d. A Mathematical Theory of Communication

7. In mathematics, a _____ is a constant multiplicative factor of a certain object. For example, in the expression $9x^2$, the _____ of x^2 is 9.

The object can be such things as a variable, a vector, a function, etc.

Chapter 3. ALGEBRAIC FUNCTIONS

   a. Coefficient
   b. Stability radius
   c. Fibonacci polynomials
   d. Multivariate division algorithm

8. In abstract algebra, a field extension L /K is called _____ if every element of L is _____ over K. Field extensions which are not _____.

For example, the field extension R/Q, that is the field of real numbers as an extension of the field of rational numbers, is transcendental, while the field extensions C/R and Q

   a. Echo
   b. Ideal
   c. Identity
   d. Algebraic

9. In mathematics, an _____ is informally a function which satisfies a polynomial equation whose coefficients are themselves polynomials. For example, an _____ in one variable x is a solution y for an equation

$$a_n(x)y^n + a_{n-1}(x)y^{n-1} + \cdots + a_0(x) = 0$$

where the coefficients a_i

   a. Alternatization
   b. Algebraic solution
   c. Algebraic signal processing
   d. Algebraic function

10. In mathematics, the _____ of a polynomial is the term of degree 0. For example, in the polynomial

   $X^3 + 2X + 3$

over the variable X, the _____ is 3. Here, the _____ is given by a numeral, but it may also be specified by a letter that is a parameter rather than a variable, as in the polynomial

   $ax^2 + bx + c$,

in the variable x, where a, b, and c are parameters so that c is the _____.

Chapter 3. ALGEBRAIC FUNCTIONS

a. Jacobian conjecture
b. Constant term
c. Sheffer sequence
d. Stability radius

11. In mathematical analysis, the _____ states that for each value between the least upper bound and greatest lower bound of the image of a continuous function there is a corresponding value in its domain mapping to the original. _____

- Version I. The _____ states the following: If the function y = f∈ [a, b] such that f

- Version II. Suppose that I is an interval [a, b] in the real numbers R and that f : I → R is a continuous function. Then the image set f

  f⊇ [f or f(I) ⊇ [f(b), f(a)].

It is frequently stated in the following equivalent form: Suppose that f : [a, b] → R is continuous and that u is a real number satisfying f(a) < u < f(b) or f(a) > u > f(b.) Then for some c ∈ [a, b], f(c) = u.

This captures an intuitive property of continuous functions: given f continuous on [1, 2], if f(1) = 3 and f(2) = 5 then f must take the value 4 somewhere between 1 and 2.

a. Intermediate Value Theorem
b. Equicontinuous
c. A Mathematical Theory of Communication
d. Uniformly continuous

12. In vascular plants, the _____ is the organ of a plant body that typically lies below the surface of the soil. This is not always the case, however, since a _____ can also be aerial (that is, growing above the ground) or aerating (that is, growing up above the ground or especially above water.) Furthermore, a stem normally occurring below ground is not exceptional either

a. 1-center problem
b. 120-cell
c. 2-3 heap
d. Root

13. In mathematics, a _____ is a statement that can be proved on the basis of explicitly stated or previously agreed assumptions.

a. Logical value
b. Disjunction introduction
c. Boolean function
d. Theorem

14. In algebra, a _____ of an element in a quadratic extension field of a field K is its image under the unique non-identity automorphism of the extended field that fixes K. If the extension is generated by a square root of an element r of K, then the _____ of $a + b\sqrt{r}$ is $a - b\sqrt{r}$ for $a, b \in K$, and in particular in the case of the field C of complex numbers as an extension of the field R of real numbers, the complex _____ of a + bi is a − bi.

Forming the sum or product of any element of the extension field with its _____ always gives an element of K.

a. Real structure
b. Relation algebra
c. Trinomial
d. Conjugate

15. In abstract algebra, a module S over a ring R is called _____ or irreducible if it is not the zero module 0 and if its only submodules are 0 and S. Understanding the _____ modules over a ring is usually helpful because these modules form the 'building blocks' of all other modules in a certain sense.

Abelian groups are the same as Z-modules.

a. Simple
b. Basis
c. Derivation
d. Harmonic series

16. In mathematics, a _____ is the end result of a division problem. It can also be expressed as the number of times the divisor divides into the dividend.

a. Limiting
b. Notation
c. Marginal cost
d. Quotient

Chapter 3. ALGEBRAIC FUNCTIONS

17. In mathematics, the _____s are an extension of the real numbers obtained by adjoining an imaginary unit, denoted i, which satisfies:

$$i^2 = -1.$$

Every _____ can be written in the form a + bi, where a and b are real numbers called the real part and the imaginary part of the _____, respectively.

_____s are a field, and thus have addition, subtraction, multiplication, and division operations. These operations extend the corresponding operations on real numbers, although with a number of additional elegant and useful properties, e.g., negative real numbers can be obtained by squaring _____s.

   a. Real part
   b. 120-cell
   c. Complex number
   d. 1-center problem

18. In mathematics, computing, linguistics and related subjects, an _____ is a sequence of finite instructions, often used for calculation and data processing. It is formally a type of effective method in which a list of well-defined instructions for completing a task will, when given an initial state, proceed through a well-defined series of successive states, eventually terminating in an end-state. The transition from one state to the next is not necessarily deterministic; some _____s, known as probabilistic _____s, incorporate randomness.
   a. Approximate counting algorithm
   b. Out-of-core
   c. Algorithm
   d. In-place algorithm

19. In mathematics, especially in the area of abstract algebra known as ring theory, a _____ is a ring with 0 ≠ 1 such that ab = 0 implies that either a = 0 or b = 0. That is, it is a nontrivial ring without left or right zero divisors. A commutative _____ is called an integral _____.
   a. Left primitive ring
   b. Modular representation theory
   c. Simple ring
   d. Domain

20. An _____ of a real-valued function y = f(x) is a curve which describes the behavior of f as either x or y tends to infinity.

In other words, as one moves along the graph of f(x) in some direction, the distance between it and the _____ eventually becomes smaller than any distance that one may specify.

If a curve A has the curve B as an _____, one says that A is asymptotic to B. Similarly B is asymptotic to A, so A and B are called asymptotic.

a. Improper integral
b. Isoperimetric dimension
c. Infinite product
d. Asymptote

21. Suppose f is a function. Then the line y = a is a _____ for f if

$$\lim_{x \to \infty} f(x) = a \text{ or } \lim_{x \to -\infty} f(x) = a.$$

Intuitively, this means that f(x) can be made as close as desired to a by making x big enough. How big is big enough depends on how close one wishes to make f(x) to a.

a. 2-3 heap
b. 1-center problem
c. 120-cell
d. Horizontal asymptote

22. When a linear asymptote is not parallel to the x- or y-axis, it is called either an oblique asymptote or equivalently a _____. The function f(x) is asymptotic to y = mx + b if

$$\lim_{x \to \infty} f(x) - (mx + b) = 0 \text{ or } \lim_{x \to -\infty} f(x) - (mx + b) = 0$$

Note that y = mx + b is never a vertical asymptote, but can be a horizontal asymptote if m=0 (in which case it is not an oblique asymptote.)

Chapter 3. ALGEBRAIC FUNCTIONS

An example is $f(x)=(x^2-1)/x$ which has an oblique asymptote of y=x (m=1, b=0) as seen in the limit

$$\lim_{x \to \infty} f(x) - x$$
$$= \lim_{x \to \infty} \frac{x^2 - 1}{x} - x$$
$$= \lim_{x \to \infty} (x - 1/x) - x$$
$$= \lim_{x \to \infty} -1/x = 0$$

Computationally identifying an oblique asymptote can be more difficult than a horizontal or vertical asymptote, in particular because the m and b might not be known.

a. 120-cell
b. 2-3 heap
c. 1-center problem
d. Slant asymptote

23. A _____ is the longest side of a right triangle, the side opposite of the right angle. The length of the _____ of a right triangle can be found using the Pythagorean theorem, which states that the square of the length of the _____ equals the sum of the squares of the lengths of the two other sides.

For example, if one of the other sides has a length of 3 meters and the other has a length of 4 m.

a. Golden angle
b. Concyclic points
c. Reflection symmetry
d. Hypotenuse

24. In mathematics, the _____ of a complex number z, is the second element of the ordered pair of real numbers representing z,. It is denoted by Im or $\Im\{z\}$, where $\Im$ is a capital I in the Fraktur typeface. The complex function which maps z to the _____ of z is not holomorphic.

a. A posteriori
b. A Mathematical Theory of Communication
c. Imaginary part
d. A chemical equation

Chapter 3. ALGEBRAIC FUNCTIONS

25. In mathematics, the _____ of a complex number z, is the first element of the ordered pair of real numbers representing z. It is denoted by Re{z} or $\mathfrak{R}${z}, where $\mathfrak{R}$ is a capital R in the Fraktur typeface. The complex function which maps z to the _____ of z is not holomorphic.

a. 1-center problem
b. 120-cell
c. Complex number
d. Real part

26. In algebra, the _____ of a polynomial with real or complex coefficients is a certain expression in the coefficients of the polynomial which is equal to zero if and only if the polynomial has a multiple root in the complex numbers. For example, the _____ of the quadratic polynomial

$$ax^2 + bx + c \text{ is } b^2 - 4ac.$$

The _____ of the cubic polynomial

$$ax^3 + bx^2 + cx + d \text{ is } b^2c^2 - 4ac^3 - 4b^3d - 27a^2d^2 + 18abcd.$$

a. Discriminant
b. Jacobian conjecture
c. Boubaker polynomial
d. Square-free polynomial

27. In mathematics, the _____ of a complex number is given by changing the sign of the imaginary part. Thus, the conjugate of the complex number

$$z = a + ib$$

(where a and b are real numbers) is

$$\bar{z} = a - ib.$$

The _____ is also very commonly denoted by z *. Here $\bar{z}$ is chosen to avoid confusion with the notation for the conjugate transpose of a matrix (which can be thought of as a generalization of complex conjugation.)

a. 120-cell
b. Complex conjugate
c. Real part
d. 1-center problem

Chapter 3. ALGEBRAIC FUNCTIONS

28. In mathematics, the _____ states that every non-constant single-variable polynomial with complex coefficients has at least one complex root. Equivalently, the field of complex numbers is algebraically closed.

Sometimes, this theorem is stated as: every non-zero single-variable polynomial, with complex coefficients, has exactly as many complex roots as its degree, if each root is counted up to its multiplicity.

 a. Distributive
 b. Closure with a twist
 c. Near-semiring
 d. Fundamental Theorem of Algebra

29. In cryptography, _____ is a pseudorandom number generator and a stream cipher designed by Robert Jenkins to be cryptographically secure. The name is an acronym for Indirection, Shift, Accumulate, Add, and Count.

The _____ algorithm has similarities with RC4.

 a. Isaac
 b. Order
 c. Imputation
 d. Introduction

30. The _____ (symbol: N) is the SI derived unit of force, named after Isaac _____ in recognition of his work on classical mechanics.

The _____ is the unit of force derived in the SI system; it is equal to the amount of force required to accelerate a mass of one kilogram at a rate of one meter per second per second. Algebraically:

$$1\text{ N} = 1\ \frac{\text{kg} \cdot \text{m}}{\text{s}^2}.$$

- 1 N is the force of Earth's gravity on an object with a mass of about 102 g ($\frac{1}{9.8}$ kg) (such as a small apple.)
- On Earth's surface, a mass of 1 kg exerts a force of approximately 9.80665 N [down] (or 1 kgf.) The approximation of 1 kg corresponding to 10 N is sometimes used as a rule of thumb in everyday life and in engineering.
- The force of Earth's gravity on a human being with a mass of 70 kg is approximately 687 N.
- The dot product of force and distance is mechanical work. Thus, in SI units, a force of 1 N exerted over a distance of 1 m is 1 NÂ·m of work. The Work-Energy Theorem states that the work done on a body is equal to the change in energy of the body. 1 NÂ·m = 1 J (joule), the SI unit of energy.
- It is common to see forces expressed in kilonewtons or kN, where 1 kN = 1 000 N.

a. 1-center problem
b. 2-3 heap
c. 120-cell
d. Newton

Chapter 4. TRIGONOMETRIC FUNCTIONS

1. In geometry and trigonometry, an _____ is the figure formed by two rays sharing a common endpoint, called the vertex of the _____. The magnitude of the _____ is the 'amount of rotation' that separates the two rays, and can be measured by considering the length of circular arc swept out when one ray is rotated about the vertex to coincide with the other. Where there is no possibility of confusion, the term '_____' is used interchangeably for both the geometric configuration itself and for its angular magnitude.
   a. A chemical equation
   b. A posteriori
   c. A Mathematical Theory of Communication
   d. Angle

2. An angle smaller than a right angle is called an _____ (less than 90 degrees).
   a. Euclidean geometry
   b. Integral geometry
   c. Ultraparallel theorem
   d. Acute angle

3. Initial objects are also called _____, and terminal objects are also called final.
   a. Colimit
   b. Terminal object
   c. Direct limit
   d. Coterminal

4. In geometry, a _____ is a special kind of point, usually a corner of a polygon, polyhedron, or higher dimensional polytope. In the geometry of curves a _____ is a point of where the first derivative of curvature is zero. In graph theory, a _____ is the fundamental unit out of which graphs are formed
   a. Duality
   b. Vertex
   c. Crib
   d. Dini

5. The _____ is a unit of plane angle, equal to 180/π degrees, or about 57.2958 degrees. It is the standard unit of angular measurement in all areas of mathematics beyond the elementary level.

The _____ is represented by the symbol 'rad' or, more rarely, by the superscript c.

a. 2-3 heap
b. 120-cell
c. 1-center problem
d. Radian

6. In mathematics the concept of a _____ generalizes notions such as 'length', 'area', and 'volume'. Informally, given some base set, a '_____' is any consistent assignment of 'sizes' to the subsets of the base set. Depending on the application, the 'size' of a subset may be interpreted as its physical size, the amount of something that lies within the subset, or the probability that some random process will yield a result within the subset.
   a. Lattice
   b. Measure
   c. Congruent
   d. Cusp

7. In mathematics, the _____ of a Euclidean space is a special point, usually denoted by the letter O, used as a fixed point of reference for the geometry of the surrounding space. In a Cartesian coordinate system, the _____ is the point where the axes of the system intersect. In Euclidean geometry, the _____ may be chosen freely as any convenient point of reference.
   a. Interval
   b. OMAC
   c. Autonomous system
   d. Origin

8. The mathematical concept of a _____ expresses the intuitive idea of deterministic dependence between two quantities, one of which is viewed as primary and the other as secondary. A _____ then is a way to associate a unique output for each input of a specified type, for example, a real number or an element of a given set.
   a. Function
   b. Coherent
   c. Grill
   d. Going up

9. In mathematics, the _____s may be described informally in several different ways. The _____s include both rational numbers, such as 42 and −23/129, and irrational numbers, such as pi and the square root of two; or, a _____ can be given by an infinite decimal representation, such as 2.4871773339...., where the digits continue in some way; or, the _____s may be thought of as points on an infinitely long number line.

These descriptions of the _____s, while intuitively accessible, are not sufficiently rigorous for the purposes of pure mathematics.

Chapter 4. TRIGONOMETRIC FUNCTIONS

a. Pre-algebra
b. Tally marks
c. Minkowski distance
d. Real number

10. In geometry and trigonometry, a _____ is defined as an angle between two straight intersecting lines of ninety degrees, or one-quarter of a circle.
  a. Trigonometry
  b. Right angle
  c. Sine integral
  d. Trigonometric functions

11. A _____ is one of the basic shapes of geometry: a polygon with three corners or vertices and three sides or edges which are line segments. A _____ with vertices A, B, and C is denoted ABC.

In Euclidean geometry any three non-collinear points determine a unique _____ and a unique plane.

  a. Kepler triangle
  b. 1-center problem
  c. Fuhrmann circle
  d. Triangle

12. _____ is a quantity expressing the two-dimensional size of a defined part of a surface, typically a region bounded by a closed curve. The term surface _____ refers to the total _____ of the exposed surface of a 3-dimensional solid, such as the sum of the _____s of the exposed sides of a polyhedron. _____ is an important invariant in the differential geometry of surfaces.
  a. Area
  b. A Mathematical Theory of Communication
  c. A posteriori
  d. A chemical equation

13. The _____ of an angle is the ratio of the length of the opposite side to the length of the hypotenuse. In our case

$$\sin A = \frac{\text{opposite}}{\text{hypotenuse}} = \frac{a}{h}.$$

Chapter 4. TRIGONOMETRIC FUNCTIONS

Note that this ratio does not depend on size of the particular right triangle chosen, as long as it contains the angle A, since all such triangles are similar.

The cosine of an angle is the ratio of the length of the adjacent side to the length of the hypotenuse.

a. Trigonometric functions
b. Law of sines
c. Right angle
d. Sine

14. In mathematics, the _____ functions are functions of an angle; they are important when studying triangles and modeling periodic phenomena, among many other applications.
a. Gudermannian function
b. Law of sines
c. Trigonometric
d. Coversine

15. In mathematics, the _____ are functions of an angle. They are important in the study of triangles and modeling periodic phenomena, among many other applications. _____ are commonly defined as ratios of two sides of a right triangle containing the angle, and can equivalently be defined as the lengths of various line segments from a unit circle.
a. Law of sines
b. Trigonometric integrals
c. Trigonometric functions
d. Sine

16. In mathematics, the _____ of a real number is its numerical value without regard to its sign. So, for example, 3 is the _____ of both 3 and −3.

The _____ of a number a is denoted by $|a|$.

Generalizations of the _____ for real numbers occur in a wide variety of mathematical settings.

a. Area hyperbolic functions
b. Absolute value
c. A chemical equation
d. A Mathematical Theory of Communication

Chapter 4. TRIGONOMETRIC FUNCTIONS

17. A _____ is a simple shape of Euclidean geometry consisting of those points in a plane which are at a constant distance, called the radius, from a fixed point, called the center. A _____ with center A is sometimes denoted by the symbol A.

A chord of a _____ is a line segment whose two endpoints lie on the _____.

   a. Circular segment
   b. Circumcircle
   c. Malfatti circles
   d. Circle

18. In mathematics, a _____ is a circle with a unit radius. Frequently, especially in trigonometry, 'the' _____ is the circle of radius 1 centered at the origin in the Cartesian coordinate system in the Euclidean plane. The _____ is often denoted S^1; the generalization to higher dimensions is the unit sphere.
   a. Unit circle
   b. Open unit disk
   c. Inscribed angle theorem
   d. Excircle

19. In mathematics, a _____ is a number that can be expressed as an integral of an algebraic function over an algebraic domain. Kontsevich and Zagier define a _____ as a complex number whose real and imaginary parts are values of absolutely convergent integrals of rational functions with rational coefficients, over domains in given by polynomial inequalities with rational coefficients.
   a. Disk
   b. Closeness
   c. Boussinesq approximation
   d. Period

20. In mathematics, a _____ is a function that repeats its values after some definite period has been added to its independent variable. This property is called periodicity. An illustration of a _____ with period P.

Everyday examples are seen when the variable is time; for instance the hands of a clock or the phases of the moon show periodic behaviour.

   a. Calculus controversy
   b. Method of indivisibles
   c. Hyperbolic angle
   d. Periodic function

21. _____ is the magnitude of change in the oscillating variable, with each oscillation, within an oscillating system. For instance, sound waves are oscillations in atmospheric pressure and their _____s are proportional to the change in pressure during one oscillation. If the variable undergoes regular oscillations, and a graph of the system is drawn with the oscillating variable as the vertical axis and time as the horizontal axis, the _____ is visually represented by the vertical distance between the extrema of the curve.
   a. Amplitude
   b. Angular velocity
   c. Areal velocity
   d. Angular frequency

22. _____ is a term in mathematics. It can refer to:

   - a _____ line, in geometry
   - the trigonometric function called _____
   - the _____ method, a root-finding algorithm in numerical analysis

   a. Solvable
   b. Secant
   c. Separable
   d. Large set

23. In trigonometry, the _____ is a function defined as $\tan x = \sin x / \cos x$. The function is so-named because it can be defined as the length of a certain segment of a _____ (in the geometric sense) to the unit circle. In plane geometry, a line is _____ to a curve, at some point, if both line and curve pass through the point with the same direction.
   a. Hopf conjectures
   b. Conformal geometry
   c. Projective connection
   d. Tangent

24. In mathematics, especially in the area of abstract algebra known as ring theory, a _____ is a ring with 0 ≠ 1 such that ab = 0 implies that either a = 0 or b = 0. That is, it is a nontrivial ring without left or right zero divisors. A commutative _____ is called an integral _____.
   a. Modular representation theory
   b. Simple ring
   c. Left primitive ring
   d. Domain

Chapter 4. TRIGONOMETRIC FUNCTIONS

25. In mathematics and in the sciences, a _____ (plural: _____e, formulæ or _____s) is a concise way of expressing information symbolically (as in a mathematical or chemical _____), or a general relationship between quantities. One of many famous _____e is Albert Einstein's E = mc² (see special relativity

In mathematics, a _____ is a key to solve an equation with variables. For example, the problem of determining the volume of a sphere is one that requires a significant amount of integral calculus to solve.

   a. 120-cell
   b. 2-3 heap
   c. 1-center problem
   d. Formula

26. _____ is an adjective meaning contiguous, adjoining or abutting.

In geometry, _____ is when sides meet to make an angle.

In trigonometry the _____ side of a right angled triangle is the cathetus next to the angle in question.

   a. Affine geometry
   b. Adjacent
   c. Ambient space
   d. Ordered geometry

27. A _____ is the longest side of a right triangle, the side opposite of the right angle. The length of the _____ of a right triangle can be found using the Pythagorean theorem, which states that the square of the length of the _____ equals the sum of the squares of the lengths of the two other sides.

For example, if one of the other sides has a length of 3 meters and the other has a length of 4 m.

   a. Concyclic points
   b. Hypotenuse
   c. Reflection symmetry
   d. Golden angle

28. In mathematics, the _____ of a number n is the number that, when added to n, yields zero. The _____ of n is denoted −n. For example, 7 is −7, because 7 + (−7) = 0, and the _____ of −0.3 is 0.3, because −0.3 + 0.3 = 0.

a. Arity
b. Additive inverse
c. Algebraic structure
d. Associativity

29. In algebraic geometry, _____ is a notion of genericity for a set of points, or other geometric objects. It means the general case situation, as opposed to some more special or coincidental cases that are possible. Its precise meaning differs in different settings.
    a. Lipschitz domain
    b. Convexity
    c. General position
    d. Compactness measure of a shape

30. In mathematics, the _____ or cyclometric functions are the so-called inverse functions of the trigonometric functions, though they do not meet the official definition for inverse functions as their domains are subsets of the images of the original functions.
    a. A posteriori
    b. A Mathematical Theory of Communication
    c. A chemical equation
    d. Inverse trigonometric functions

31. In trigonometry, the _____ is a statement about a general triangle which relates the lengths of its sides to the cosine of one of its angles. Using notation as in Fig. 1, the _____ states that

$$c^2 = a^2 + b^2 - 2ab\cos(\gamma),$$

or, equivalently:

$$b^2 = c^2 + a^2 - 2ca\cos(\beta),$$
$$a^2 = b^2 + c^2 - 2bc\cos(\alpha),$$
$$\cos(\gamma) = \frac{a^2 + b^2 - c^2}{2ab}.$$

Note that c is the side opposite of angle γ, and that a and b are the two sides enclosing γ.

a. Trigonometric
b. Law of tangents
c. Trigonometric functions
d. Law of cosines

32. The _____, in trigonometry, is a statement about any triangle in a plane. Where the sides of the triangle are a, b and c and the angles opposite those sides are A, B and C, then the _____ states equality of the first three quantities below:

$$\underbrace{\frac{a}{\sin A} = \frac{b}{\sin B} = \frac{c}{\sin C}}_{\text{Law of sines}} = 2R$$

where R is the radius of the triangle's circumcircle. The _____ is also sometimes stated as

$$\frac{\sin A}{a} = \frac{\sin B}{b} = \frac{\sin C}{c}.$$

This law is useful when computing the remaining sides of a triangle if two angles and a side are known, a common problem in the technique of triangulation.

a. Sine integral
b. Law of sines
c. Trigonometric functions
d. Trigonometric

33. In statistics the _____ of an event i is the number n_i of times the event occurred in the experiment or the study. These frequencies are often graphically represented in histograms.

We speak of absolute frequencies, when the counts n_i themselves are given and of

$$f_i = \frac{n_i}{N} = \frac{n_i}{\sum_i n_i}$$

Taking the f_i for all i and tabulating or plotting them leads to a _____ distribution.

Chapter 4. TRIGONOMETRIC FUNCTIONS

   a. Digital room correction
   b. Frequency
   c. Robinson-Dadson curves
   d. Subharmonic

34. In acoustics and telecommunication, the _____ of a wave is a component frequency of the signal that is an integer multiple of the fundamental frequency. For example, if the frequency is f, the _____s have frequency 2f, 3f, 4f, etc, as well as f itself. The _____s have the property that they are all periodic at the signal frequency.
   a. Subharmonic
   b. Robinson-Dadson curves
   c. Digital room correction
   d. Harmonic

35. In abstract algebra, a module S over a ring R is called _____ or irreducible if it is not the zero module 0 and if its only submodules are 0 and S. Understanding the _____ modules over a ring is usually helpful because these modules form the 'building blocks' of all other modules in a certain sense.

Abelian groups are the same as Z-modules.

   a. Derivation
   b. Simple
   c. Harmonic series
   d. Basis

36. _____ is the motion of a simple harmonic oscillator, a motion that is neither driven nor damped. The motion is periodic, as it repeats itself at standard intervals in a specific manner - described as being sinusoidal, with constant amplitude. It is characterized by its amplitude, its period which is the time for a single oscillation, its frequency which is the number of cycles per unit time, and its phase, which determines the starting point on the sine wave.
   a. Configuration space
   b. Stretch rule
   c. Kinematics
   d. Simple harmonic motion

37. In combinatorial mathematics, a _____ is an un-ordered collection of distinct elements, usually of a prescribed size and taken from a given set. Given such a set S, a _____ of elements of S is just a subset of S, where as always forsets the order of the elements is not taken into account. Also, as always forsets, no elements can be repeated more than once in a _____; this is often referred to as a 'collection without repetition'.

a. Fill-in
b. Combination
c. Heawood number
d. Sparsity

38. The _____ is the length of the line that bounds an area In the special case where the area is circular, the _____ is known as the circumference.

a. Reflection symmetry
b. Concyclic
c. Multilateration
d. Perimeter

Chapter 5. EXPONENTIAL AND LOGARITHM FUNCTIONS

1. The mathematical concept of a _____ expresses the intuitive idea of deterministic dependence between two quantities, one of which is viewed as primary and the other as secondary. A _____ then is a way to associate a unique output for each input of a specified type, for example, a real number or an element of a given set.
    a. Coherent
    b. Function
    c. Going up
    d. Grill

2. In mathematics, the _____ of a real number is its numerical value without regard to its sign. So, for example, 3 is the _____ of both 3 and −3.

    The _____ of a number a is denoted by | a | .

    Generalizations of the _____ for real numbers occur in a wide variety of mathematical settings.

    a. A Mathematical Theory of Communication
    b. Absolute value
    c. Area hyperbolic functions
    d. A chemical equation

3. The _____ is a function in mathematics. The application of this function to a value x is written as ex. Equivalently, this can be written in the form e^x, where e is a mathematical constant, the base of the natural logarithm, which equals approximately 2.718281828, and is also known as Euler's number.
    a. Exponential Function
    b. A Mathematical Theory of Communication
    c. Area hyperbolic functions
    d. A chemical equation

4. In mathematics and computer science, _____ (also base-16, hexa or base, of 16. It uses sixteen distinct symbols, most often the symbols 0-9 to represent values zero to nine, and A, B, C, D, E, F (or a through f) to represent values ten to fifteen.

    Its primary use is as a human friendly representation of binary coded values, so it is often used in digital electronics and computer engineering.

    a. Hexadecimal
    b. Factoradic
    c. Radix
    d. Tetradecimal

Chapter 5. EXPONENTIAL AND LOGARITHM FUNCTIONS

5. A _____ is a software program that facilitates symbolic mathematics. The core functionality of a CAS is manipulation of mathematical expressions in symbolic form.

The symbolic manipulations supported typically include

- simplification to the smallest possible expression or some standard form, including automatic simplification with assumptions and simplification with constraints
- substitution of symbolic, functors or numeric values for expressions
- change of form of expressions: expanding products and powers, partial and full factorization, rewriting as partial fractions, constraint satisfaction, rewriting trigonometric functions as exponentials, etc.
- partial and total differentiation
- symbolic constrained and unconstrained global optimization
- solution of linear and some non-linear equations over various domains
- solution of some differential and difference equations
- taking some limits
- some indefinite and definite integration, including multidimensional integrals
- integral transforms
- arbitrary-precision numeric operations
- Series operations such as expansion, summation and products
- matrix operations including products, inverses, etc.
- display of mathematical expressions in two-dimensional mathematical form, often using typesetting systems similar to TeX
- add-ons for use in applied mathematics such as physics packages for physical computation
- plotting graphs and parametric plots of functions in two and three dimensions, and animating them
- APIs for linking it on an external program such as a database, or using in a programming language to use the _____
- drawing charts and diagrams
- string manipulation such as matching and searching
- statistical computation
- Theorem proving and verification
- graphic production and editing such as CGI and signal processing as image processing
- sound synthesis

Many also include a programming language, allowing users to implement their own algorithms.

Some _____s focus on a specific area of application; these are typically developed in academia and are free.

a. 2-3 heap
b. Computer algebra system
c. 120-cell
d. 1-center problem

Chapter 5. EXPONENTIAL AND LOGARITHM FUNCTIONS

6. In mathematics and in the sciences, a _____ (plural: _____e, formulæ or _____s) is a concise way of expressing information symbolically (as in a mathematical or chemical _____), or a general relationship between quantities. One of many famous _____e is Albert Einstein's E = mc² (see special relativity

In mathematics, a _____ is a key to solve an equation with variables. For example, the problem of determining the volume of a sphere is one that requires a significant amount of integral calculus to solve.

 a. 2-3 heap
 b. 120-cell
 c. Formula
 d. 1-center problem

7. In mathematics, the _____s may be described informally in several different ways. The _____s include both rational numbers, such as 42 and −23/129, and irrational numbers, such as pi and the square root of two; or, a _____ can be given by an infinite decimal representation, such as 2.4871773339...., where the digits continue in some way; or, the _____s may be thought of as points on an infinitely long number line.

These descriptions of the _____s, while intuitively accessible, are not sufficiently rigorous for the purposes of pure mathematics.

 a. Real number
 b. Tally marks
 c. Pre-algebra
 d. Minkowski distance

8. In mathematics, a _____ is the end result of a division problem. It can also be expressed as the number of times the divisor divides into the dividend.
 a. Limiting
 b. Marginal cost
 c. Quotient
 d. Notation

9. In mathematics, the concept of a _____ tries to capture the intuitive idea of a geometrical one-dimensional and continuous object. A simple example is the circle. In everyday use of the term '_____', a straight line is not curved, but in mathematical parlance _____s include straight lines and line segments.

Chapter 5. EXPONENTIAL AND LOGARITHM FUNCTIONS

a. Quadrifolium
b. Kappa curve
c. Curve
d. Negative pedal curve

10. _____ is the concept of adding accumulated interest back to the principal, so that interest is earned on interest from that moment on. The act of declaring interest to be principal is called compounding. A loan, for example, may have its interest compounded every month: in this case, a loan with $100 principal and 1% interest per month would have a balance of $101 at the end of the first month.

a. Retained interest
b. Net interest margin
c. Net interest margin securities
d. Compound interest

11. _____ is a fee, paid on borrowed capital. Assets lent include money, shares, consumer goods through hire purchase, major assets such as aircraft, and even entire factories in finance lease arrangements. The _____ is calculated upon the value of the assets in the same manner as upon money.

a. Interest sensitivity gap
b. Interest expense
c. A Mathematical Theory of Communication
d. Interest

12. In mathematics, the _____ of a number to a given base is the power or exponent to which the base must be raised in order to produce the number.

For example, the _____ of 1000 to the base 10 is 3, because 3 is how many 10s one must multiply to get 1000: thus 10 × 10 × 10 = 1000; the base-2 _____ of 32 is 5 because 5 is how many 2s one must multiply to get 32: thus 2 × 2 × 2 × 2 × 2 = 32. In the language of exponents: 10^3 = 1000, so $\log_{10} 1000 = 3$, and $2^5 = 32$, so $\log_2 32 = 5$.

a. 1-center problem
b. 2-3 heap
c. Logarithm
d. 120-cell

Chapter 5. EXPONENTIAL AND LOGARITHM FUNCTIONS

13. The function $\log_b(x)$ depends on both b and x, but the term _____ (or logarithmic function) in standard usage refers to a function of the form $\log_b(x)$ in which the base b is fixed and so the only argument is x. Thus there is one _____ for each value of the base b (which must be positive and must differ from 1.) Viewed in this way, the base-b _____ is the inverse function of the exponential function b^x.
   a. Logarithm Function
   b. 120-cell
   c. 1-center problem
   d. 2-3 heap

14. The _____, formerly known as the hyperbolic logarithm, is the logarithm to the base e, where e is an irrational constant approximately equal to 2.718 281 828. It is also sometimes referred to as the Napierian logarithm, although the original meaning of this term is slightly different. In simple terms, the _____ of a number x is the power to which e would have to be raised to equal x -- for example the natural log of e itself is 1 because e^1 = e, while the _____ of 1 would be 0, since e^0 = 1.
   a. Natural logarithm
   b. 1-center problem
   c. Logarithmic identities
   d. Logarithmic growth

15. The _____ is the logarithm with base 10. It is also known as the decadic logarithm, named after its base. It is indicated by $\log_{10}$
   a. 1-center problem
   b. Natural logarithm
   c. Common logarithm
   d. Logarithmic growth

16. The _____ is a unit of plane angle, equal to 180/π degrees, or about 57.2958 degrees. It is the standard unit of angular measurement in all areas of mathematics beyond the elementary level.

The _____ is represented by the symbol 'rad' or, more rarely, by the superscript c.

   a. Radian
   b. 120-cell
   c. 1-center problem
   d. 2-3 heap

Chapter 5. EXPONENTIAL AND LOGARITHM FUNCTIONS

17. _____ is the change in population over time, and can be quantified as the change in the number of individuals in a population using 'per unit time' for measurement. The term _____ can technically refer to any species, but almost always refers to humans, and it is often used informally for the more specific demographic term _____ rate, and is often used to refer specifically to the growth of the population of the world.

Simple models of _____ include the Malthusian Growth Model and the logistic model.

a. 120-cell
b. Population dynamics
c. 1-center problem
d. Population growth

18. _____ is the process in which an unstable atomic nucleus loses energy by emitting ionizing particles and radiation. This decay, or loss of energy, results in an atom of one type, called the parent nuclide transforming to an atom of a different type, called the daughter nuclide. For example: a carbon-14 atom emits radiation and transforms to a nitrogen-14 atom.

a. 1-center problem
b. Radioactive decay
c. Half-life
d. 120-cell

19. A quantity is said to be subject to _____ if it decreases at a rate proportional to its value. Symbolically, this can be expressed as the following differential equation, where N is the quantity and λ is a positive number called the decay constant.

$$\frac{dN}{dt} = -\lambda N.$$

The solution to this equation is:

$$N(t) = N_0 e^{-\lambda t}.$$

Here is the quantity at time t, and $N_0 = N$ is the quantity, at time t = 0.

a. Exponential formula
b. Exponentiating by squaring
c. Exponential integral
d. Exponential decay

Chapter 5. EXPONENTIAL AND LOGARITHM FUNCTIONS

20. _____ occurs when the growth rate of a mathematical function is proportional to the function's current value. In the case of a discrete domain of definition with equal intervals it is also called geometric growth or geometric decay.

With _____ of a positive value its rate of increase steadily increases, or in the case of exponential decay, its rate of decrease steadily decreases.

a. A Mathematical Theory of Communication
b. Exponential growth
c. A posteriori
d. A chemical equation

21. _____ is a special mathematical relationship between two quantities.Two quantities are called proportional if they vary in such a way that one of the quantities is a constant multiple of the other, or equivalently if they have a constant ratio.
a. Compression
b. Discontinuity
c. Proportionality
d. Depth

22. The _____ of a quantity whose value decreases with time is the interval required for the quantity to decay to half of its initial value. The concept originated in describing how long it takes atoms to undergo radioactive decay, but also applies in a wide variety of other situations.

The term '_____' dates to 1907.

a. 1-center problem
b. Radioactive decay
c. 120-cell
d. Half-life

23. In physics and geometry, the _____ is the theoretical shape of a hanging flexible chain or cable when supported at its ends and acted upon by a uniform gravitational force and in equilibrium. The curve has a U shape that is similar in appearance to the parabola, though it is a different curve.

The word _____ is derived from the Latin word catena, which means 'chain'.

Chapter 5. EXPONENTIAL AND LOGARITHM FUNCTIONS

a. 120-cell
b. 2-3 heap
c. Catenary
d. 1-center problem

24. A _____ or logistic curve is the most common sigmoid curve. It models the S-curve of growth of some set P, where P might be thought of as population. The initial stage of growth is approximately exponential; then, as saturation begins, the growth slows, and at maturity, growth stops.
   a. Spin-weighted spherical harmonics
   b. Jack function
   c. Legendre forms
   d. Logistic function

25. The _____ of an angle is the ratio of the length of the opposite side to the length of the hypotenuse. In our case

$$\sin A = \frac{\text{opposite}}{\text{hypotenuse}} = \frac{a}{h}.$$

Note that this ratio does not depend on size of the particular right triangle chosen, as long as it contains the angle A, since all such triangles are similar.

The cosine of an angle is the ratio of the length of the adjacent side to the length of the hypotenuse.

   a. Trigonometric functions
   b. Right angle
   c. Law of sines
   d. Sine

60 Chapter 6. CONIC SECTIONS, POLAR COORDINATES, AND PARAMETRIC EQUATIONS

1. In mathematics, a _____ is a curve obtained by intersecting a cone with a plane. A _____ is therefore a restriction of a quadric surface to the plane. The _____s were named and studied as long ago as 200 BC, when Apollonius of Perga undertook a systematic study of their properties.
    a. Conic section
    b. Dandelin sphere
    c. Directrix
    d. Parabola

2. In mathematics, a _____ is a polynomial equation of the second degree. The general form is

$$ax^2 + bx + c = 0,$$

where a ≠ 0.

The letters a, b, and c are called coefficients: the quadratic coefficient a is the coefficient of x^2, the linear coefficient b is the coefficient of x, and c is the constant coefficient, also called the free term or constant term.

   a. Difference of two squares
   b. Linear equation
   c. Quartic equation
   d. Quadratic equation

3. _____ Galilei (15 February 1564 - 8 January 1642) was a Tuscan physicist, mathematician, astronomer, and philosopher who played a major role in the Scientific Revolution. His achievements include improvements to the telescope and consequent astronomical observations, and support for Copernicanism. _____ has been called the 'father of modern observational astronomy', the 'father of modern physics', the 'father of science', and 'the Father of Modern Science.' The motion of uniformly accelerated objects, taught in nearly all high school and introductory college physics courses, was studied by _____ as the subject of kinematics.
   a. Jan Kowalewski
   b. David Naccache
   c. Galileo
   d. Francesco Severi

4. In cryptography, _____ is a pseudorandom number generator and a stream cipher designed by Robert Jenkins to be cryptographically secure. The name is an acronym for Indirection, Shift, Accumulate, Add, and Count.

The _____ algorithm has similarities with RC4.

Chapter 6. CONIC SECTIONS, POLAR COORDINATES, AND PARAMETRIC EQUATIONS

a. Imputation
b. Introduction
c. Order
d. Isaac

5. The _____ (symbol: N) is the SI derived unit of force, named after Isaac _____ in recognition of his work on classical mechanics.

The _____ is the unit of force derived in the SI system; it is equal to the amount of force required to accelerate a mass of one kilogram at a rate of one meter per second per second. Algebraically:

$$1 \text{ N} = 1 \ \frac{\text{kg} \cdot \text{m}}{\text{s}^2}.$$

- 1 N is the force of Earth's gravity on an object with a mass of about 102 g ($\frac{1}{9.8}$ kg) (such as a small apple.)
- On Earth's surface, a mass of 1 kg exerts a force of approximately 9.80665 N [down] (or 1 kgf.) The approximation of 1 kg corresponding to 10 N is sometimes used as a rule of thumb in everyday life and in engineering.
- The force of Earth's gravity on a human being with a mass of 70 kg is approximately 687 N.
- The dot product of force and distance is mechanical work. Thus, in SI units, a force of 1 N exerted over a distance of 1 m is 1 NÂ·m of work. The Work-Energy Theorem states that the work done on a body is equal to the change in energy of the body. 1 NÂ·m = 1 J (joule), the SI unit of energy.
- It is common to see forces expressed in kilonewtons or kN, where 1 kN = 1 000 N.

a. 1-center problem
b. 120-cell
c. 2-3 heap
d. Newton

6. The latus rectum (2l) is the chord parallel to the _____ and passing through the focus (or one of the two foci.)

The semi-latus rectum (l) is half the latus rectum.

The focal parameter (p) is the distance from the focus (or one of the two foci) to the _____.

Chapter 6. CONIC SECTIONS, POLAR COORDINATES, AND PARAMETRIC EQUATIONS

   a. Conic section
   b. Parabola
   c. Matrix representation of conic sections
   d. Directrix

7. In mathematics, the _____ is a conic section, the intersection of a right circular conical surface and a plane parallel to a generating straight line of that surface. Given a point and a line that lie in a plane, the locus of points in that plane that are equidistant to them is a _____.

A particular case arises when the plane is tangent to the conical surface of a circle.

   a. Directrix
   b. Matrix representation of conic sections
   c. Parabola
   d. Dandelin sphere

8. In geometry, a _____ is a special kind of point, usually a corner of a polygon, polyhedron, or higher dimensional polytope. In the geometry of curves a _____ is a point of where the first derivative of curvature is zero. In graph theory, a _____ is the fundamental unit out of which graphs are formed
   a. Dini
   b. Crib
   c. Duality
   d. Vertex

9. In geometry and trigonometry, an _____ is the figure formed by two rays sharing a common endpoint, called the vertex of the _____. The magnitude of the _____ is the 'amount of rotation' that separates the two rays, and can be measured by considering the length of circular arc swept out when one ray is rotated about the vertex to coincide with the other. Where there is no possibility of confusion, the term '_____' is used interchangeably for both the geometric configuration itself and for its angular magnitude.
   a. A posteriori
   b. A Mathematical Theory of Communication
   c. A chemical equation
   d. Angle

10. In mathematics an _____ , a 'falling short') is a conic section, the locus of points in a plane such that the sum of the distances to two fixed points is equal to a given constant. The two fixed points are then called foci.

Chapter 6. CONIC SECTIONS, POLAR COORDINATES, AND PARAMETRIC EQUATIONS

Another way to define it as the path traced out by a point whose distance from a focus maintains a constant ratio less than one with its distance from a straight line not passing through the focus, called the directrix.

a. A Mathematical Theory of Communication
b. A chemical equation
c. A posteriori
d. Ellipse

11. In mathematics, a _____ is a quadric surface of special kind. There are two kinds of _____s: elliptic and hyperbolic. The elliptic _____ is shaped like an oval cup and can have a maximum or minimum point.

a. Paraboloid
b. Spheroid
c. Homoeoid
d. Dupin cyclide

12. In geometry, the semi-_____ (also semimajor axis) is used to describe the dimensions of ellipses and hyperbolae.

The _____ of an ellipse is its longest diameter, a line that runs through the centre and both foci, its ends being at the widest points of the shape. The semi-_____ is one half of the _____, and thus runs from the centre, through a focus, and to the edge of the ellipse.

a. Lagrangian points
b. Lagrange points
c. Semi-major axis
d. Major axis

13. In linear algebra, a _____ of a matrix A is the determinant of some smaller square matrix, cut down from A by removing one or more of its rows or columns.

_____s obtained by removing just one row and one column from square matrices are required for calculating matrix cofactors, which in turn are useful for computing both the determinant and inverse of square matrices.

Let A be an m × n matrix and k an integer with 0 < k ≤ m, and k ≤ n.

Chapter 6. CONIC SECTIONS, POLAR COORDINATES, AND PARAMETRIC EQUATIONS

   a. Block size
   b. Homogeneity
   c. Chiral
   d. Minor

14. In physics, an _____ is the gravitationally curved path of one object around a point or another body, for example the gravitational _____ of a planet around a star.

Historically, the apparent motion of the planets were first understood in terms of epicycles, which are the sums of numerous circular motions. This predicted the path of the planets quite well, until Johannes Kepler was able to show that the motion of the planets were in fact elliptical motions.

   a. A Mathematical Theory of Communication
   b. Orbital resonance
   c. Equatorial coordinate system
   d. Orbit

15. An _____ of a real-valued function y = f(x) is a curve which describes the behavior of f as either x or y tends to infinity.

In other words, as one moves along the graph of f(x) in some direction, the distance between it and the _____ eventually becomes smaller than any distance that one may specify.

If a curve A has the curve B as an _____, one says that A is asymptotic to B. Similarly B is asymptotic to A, so A and B are called asymptotic.

   a. Asymptote
   b. Improper integral
   c. Infinite product
   d. Isoperimetric dimension

16. When a linear asymptote is not parallel to the x- or y-axis, it is called either an oblique asymptote or equivalently a _____. The function f(x) is asymptotic to y = mx + b if

$$\lim_{x \to \infty} f(x) - (mx + b) = 0 \text{ or } \lim_{x \to -\infty} f(x) - (mx + b) = 0$$

Note that y = mx + b is never a vertical asymptote, but can be a horizontal asymptote if m=0 (in which case it is not an oblique asymptote.)

Chapter 6. CONIC SECTIONS, POLAR COORDINATES, AND PARAMETRIC EQUATIONS

An example is $f(x)=(x^2-1)/x$ which has an oblique asymptote of y=x (m=1, b=0) as seen in the limit

$$\lim_{x\to\infty} f(x) - x$$
$$= \lim_{x\to\infty} \frac{x^2-1}{x} - x$$
$$= \lim_{x\to\infty} (x - 1/x) - x$$
$$= \lim_{x\to\infty} -1/x = 0$$

Computationally identifying an oblique asymptote can be more difficult than a horizontal or vertical asymptote, in particular because the m and b might not be known.

a. 120-cell
b. Slant asymptote
c. 1-center problem
d. 2-3 heap

17. In algebra, a _____ of an element in a quadratic extension field of a field K is its image under the unique non-identity automorphism of the extended field that fixes K. If the extension is generated by a square root of an element r of K, then the _____ of $a + b\sqrt{r}$ is $a - b\sqrt{r}$ for $a, b \in K$, and in particular in the case of the field C of complex numbers as an extension of the field R of real numbers, the complex _____ of a + bi is a − bi.

Forming the sum or product of any element of the extension field with its _____ always gives an element of K.

a. Real structure
b. Trinomial
c. Relation algebra
d. Conjugate

18. In mathematics, the _____ system is a two-dimensional coordinate system in which each point on a plane is determined by an angle and a distance. The _____ system is especially useful in situations where the relationship between two points is most easily expressed in terms of angles and distance; in the more familiar Cartesian or rectangular coordinate system, such a relationship can only be found through trigonometric formulation.

As the coordinate system is two-dimensional, each point is determined by two _____s: the radial coordinate and the angular coordinate.

Chapter 6. CONIC SECTIONS, POLAR COORDINATES, AND PARAMETRIC EQUATIONS

a. Sir Isaac Newton
b. Vampire
c. Polar coordinate
d. Sequence alignment

19. In mathematics, the _____ is a two-dimensional coordinate system in which each point on a plane is determined by an angle and a distance. The _____ is especially useful in situations where the relationship between two points is most easily expressed in terms of angles and distance; in the more familiar Cartesian or rectangular coordinate system, such a relationship can only be found through trigonometric formulation.

As the coordinate system is two-dimensional, each point is determined by two polar coordinates: the radial coordinate and the angular coordinate.

a. ROT13
b. Sir Isaac Newton
c. Marian Adam Rejewski
d. Polar coordinate system

20. In complex analysis, a _____ of a meromorphic function is a certain type of singularity that behaves like the singularity $1/z^n$ at $z = 0$. This means that, in particular, a _____ of the function f

Formally, suppose U is an open subset of the complex plane C, a is an element of U and f : U − {a} → C is a function which is holomorphic over its domain.

a. Decidable
b. Pole
c. Harmonic series
d. Dini

21. The _____ is a unit of plane angle, equal to 180/π degrees, or about 57.2958 degrees. It is the standard unit of angular measurement in all areas of mathematics beyond the elementary level.

The _____ is represented by the symbol 'rad' or, more rarely, by the superscript c.

a. 120-cell
b. 2-3 heap
c. 1-center problem
d. Radian

Chapter 6. CONIC SECTIONS, POLAR COORDINATES, AND PARAMETRIC EQUATIONS

22. _____ is closed curve with one cusp.

In geometry, the _____ is an epicycloid with one cusp.

Rolling circle around another fixed circle produces _____ Conformal mapping from circle to _____

- epicycloid produced as the path of a point on the circumference of a circle as that circle rolls around another fixed circle with the same radius.
- limaçon with one cusp. The cusp is formed when the ratio of a to b in the equation is equal to one.

a. 120-cell
b. 2-3 heap
c. 1-center problem
d. Cardioid

23. A _____ is a simple shape of Euclidean geometry consisting of those points in a plane which are at a constant distance, called the radius, from a fixed point, called the center. A _____ with center A is sometimes denoted by the symbol A.

A chord of a _____ is a line segment whose two endpoints lie on the _____.

a. Malfatti circles
b. Circle
c. Circumcircle
d. Circular segment

24. In mathematics, _____ are a method of defining a curve. A simple kinematical example is when one uses a time parameter to determine the position, velocity, and other information about a body in motion.

Abstractly, a relation is given in the form of an equation, and it is shown also to be the image of functions from items such as R^n.

a. Differential operator
b. Parametric equations
c. Laplace operator
d. Multipole moment

Chapter 6. CONIC SECTIONS, POLAR COORDINATES, AND PARAMETRIC EQUATIONS

25. In mathematics, the _____ of a Euclidean space is a special point, usually denoted by the letter O, used as a fixed point of reference for the geometry of the surrounding space. In a Cartesian coordinate system, the _____ is the point where the axes of the system intersect. In Euclidean geometry, the _____ may be chosen freely as any convenient point of reference.
    a. Autonomous system
    b. Interval
    c. OMAC
    d. Origin

26. _____ generally conveys two primary meanings. The first is an imprecise sense of harmonious or aesthetically-pleasing proportionality and balance; such that it reflects beauty or perfection. The second meaning is a precise and well-defined concept of balance or 'patterned self-similarity' that can be demonstrated or proved according to the rules of a formal system: by geometry, through physics or otherwise.
    a. Symmetry breaking
    b. Tessellation
    c. Molecular symmetry
    d. Symmetry

27. The _____ is the horizontal axis of a two-dimensional plot in the Cartesian coordinate system, that is typically pointed to the right. Also known as a right-handed coordinate system.
    a. 120-cell
    b. 2-3 heap
    c. 1-center problem
    d. X-axis

28. In reference to a 2D and 3D plane, the _____ is the vertical height of a 2D or 3D object.
    a. Y-axis
    b. 120-cell
    c. 2-3 heap
    d. 1-center problem

29. In mathematics, a _____ or rhodonea curve is a sinusoid plotted in polar coordinates. Up to similarity, these curves can all be expressed by a polar equation of the form

$$r = \cos(k\theta).$$

Chapter 6. CONIC SECTIONS, POLAR COORDINATES, AND PARAMETRIC EQUATIONS

If k is an integer, the curve will be _____ shaped with

- 2k petals if k is even, and
- k petals if k is odd.

When k is even, the entire graph of the _____ will be traced out exactly once when the value of θ changes from 0 to 2π. When k is odd, this will happen on the interval between 0 and π.

If k is rational, then the curve is closed and has finite length.

a. Conchoid
b. Sextic plane curve
c. Rose
d. Cycloid

30. A _____ is the curve defined by the path of a point on the edge of circular wheel as the wheel rolls along a straight line. It is an example of a roulette, a curve generated by a curve rolling on another curve.

The _____ is the solution to the brachistochrone problem and the related tautochrone problem.

a. Superformula
b. Hippopede
c. Cycloid
d. Hessian curve

31. In Geometry, the _____ is an algebraic curve defined by the equation

$$x^3 + y^3 - 3axy = 0$$

It forms a loop in the first quadrant with a double point at the origin and asymptote

$$x + y + a = 0$$

It is symmetrical about y = x.

Chapter 6. CONIC SECTIONS, POLAR COORDINATES, AND PARAMETRIC EQUATIONS

a. Sextic plane curve
b. Trisectrix
c. Quadratrix
d. Folium of Descartes

32. In geometry, a _____ is a special plane curve generated by the trace of a fixed point on a small circle that rolls within a larger circle. It is comparable to the cycloid but instead of the circle rolling along a line, it rolls within a circle. The red curve is a _____ traced as the smaller black circle rolls around inside the larger blue circle, giving a deltoid.

If the smaller circle has radius r, and the larger circle has radius R = kr, then the parametric equations for the curve can be given by

$$x(\theta) = r(k-1)\left(\cos\theta + \frac{\cos((k-1)\theta)}{k-1}\right),$$

$$y(\theta) = r(k-1)\left(\sin\theta - \frac{\sin((k-1)\theta)}{k-1}\right).$$

If k is an integer, then the curve is closed, and has k cusps.

a. Singular point
b. Hypocycloid
c. Sextic plane curve
d. Curve

33. In geometry, an _____ is a plane curve produced by tracing the path of a chosen point of a circle -- called epicycle -- which rolls without slipping around a fixed circle. It is a particular kind of roulette.

If the smaller circle has radius r, and the larger circle has radius R = kr, then the parametric equations for the curve can be given by:

$$x(\theta) = r(k+1)\left(\cos\theta - \frac{\cos((k+1)\theta)}{k+1}\right)$$

$$y(\theta) = r(k+1)\left(\sin\theta - \frac{\sin((k+1)\theta)}{k+1}\right).$$

If k is an integer, then the curve is closed, and has k cusps.

Chapter 6. CONIC SECTIONS, POLAR COORDINATES, AND PARAMETRIC EQUATIONS

a. Algebraic curve
b. Epispiral
c. Oval
d. Epicycloid

34. In trigonometry, the _____ is a function defined as $\tan x = \sin x / \cos x$. The function is so-named because it can be defined as the length of a certain segment of a _____ (in the geometric sense) to the unit circle. In plane geometry, a line is _____ to a curve, at some point, if both line and curve pass through the point with the same direction.
   a. Conformal geometry
   b. Hopf conjectures
   c. Tangent
   d. Projective connection

35. In geometry, the _____ to a curve at a given point is the straight line that 'just touches' the curve at that point. As it passes through the point of tangency, the _____ is 'going in the same direction' as the curve, and in this sense it is the best straight-line approximation to the curve at that point. The same definition applies to space curves and curves in n-dimensional Euclidean space.
   a. Four-vertex theorem
   b. Chern-Weil theory
   c. Darboux frame
   d. Tangent line

Chapter 1

1. d	2. d	3. d	4. a	5. c	6. a	7. c	8. a	9. b	10. d
11. c	12. d	13. d	14. c	15. a	16. b	17. d	18. d	19. d	20. c
21. c	22. d	23. d	24. d	25. d	26. d	27. b	28. d	29. d	30. c
31. d	32. b	33. d	34. d	35. b	36. d	37. b	38. d	39. d	40. d
41. b	42. c	43. c	44. b	45. d	46. d	47. b	48. b	49. d	50. d
51. a	52. c	53. a	54. d	55. d	56. d	57. c	58. b	59. a	60. b
61. d	62. d	63. b	64. a	65. d	66. b	67. a	68. d	69. d	70. d
71. c	72. d	73. d	74. d						

Chapter 2

1. b	2. c	3. d	4. d	5. a	6. d	7. d	8. b	9. a	10. c
11. d	12. d	13. b	14. d	15. b	16. c	17. c	18. a	19. c	20. d
21. b	22. d								

Chapter 3

1. d	2. d	3. a	4. d	5. d	6. b	7. a	8. d	9. d	10. b
11. a	12. d	13. d	14. d	15. a	16. d	17. c	18. c	19. d	20. d
21. d	22. d	23. d	24. c	25. d	26. a	27. b	28. d	29. a	30. d

Chapter 4

1. d	2. d	3. d	4. b	5. d	6. b	7. d	8. a	9. d	10. b
11. d	12. a	13. d	14. c	15. c	16. b	17. d	18. a	19. d	20. d
21. a	22. b	23. d	24. d	25. d	26. b	27. b	28. b	29. c	30. d
31. d	32. b	33. b	34. d	35. b	36. d	37. b	38. d		

Chapter 5

1. b	2. b	3. a	4. a	5. b	6. c	7. a	8. c	9. c	10. d
11. d	12. c	13. a	14. a	15. c	16. a	17. d	18. b	19. d	20. b
21. c	22. d	23. c	24. d	25. d					

Chapter 6

1. a	2. d	3. c	4. d	5. d	6. d	7. c	8. d	9. d	10. d
11. a	12. d	13. d	14. d	15. a	16. b	17. d	18. c	19. d	20. b
21. d	22. d	23. b	24. b	25. d	26. d	27. d	28. a	29. c	30. c
31. d	32. b	33. d	34. c	35. d					

www.ingramcontent.com/pod-product-compliance
Lightning Source LLC
Chambersburg PA
CBHW081850230426
43669CB00018B/2890